# Law for Leaders™

The Roadmap Every Leader Needs to Know
to Avoid Workplace Claims and Lawsuits

## Pam Howland

### Contributors:

Benjamin T. Cramer, Doug Plass, Jennifer M. Walrath

The author can be reached at phowland@idemploymentlawyers.com.

Cover design by Prominence Publishing. Published by Prominence Publishing.

Law For Leaders™/Howland, Pam. -- 1st ed.

ISBN: 978-1-990830-73-0

# Table of Contents

Preface...........................................................................................................1

Introduction...................................................................................................5

Chapter 1: Why Supervisors Need More Training and What
That Training Looks Like ............................................................9

Chapter 2: What Does it Mean to Be an At-Will Employee and
Why You Need to Know the Answer to That Question ...........11

Chapter 3: Why You Need to Document Performance Issues and
What Your Documentation Needs to Say ................................15

Chapter 4: Discipline and Termination .........................................21

Chapter 5: Why Continual Training on Discrimination and
Harassment is Needed ...............................................................27

Chapter 6: Workplace Discrimination and Harassment—
Contributing Author Jennifer M. Walrath.................................29

Chapter 7: What to Do When a Report Comes In .........................37

Chapter 8: ADA Scope and Three Basic ADA Concepts Every
Leader Needs to Know ...............................................................43

Chapter 9: Alcoholism and Drug Addiction .................................55

Chapter 10: Mental Health and Complex Issues Like Suicide.........69

Chapter 11: The Pregnant Workers Fairness Act ............................73

Chapter 12: Equal Pay Claims ........................................................79

Chapter 13: Retaliation ...................................................................83

Chapter 14: Wage and Hour Issues—Contributing Author
Benjamin T. Cramer.................................................................87

Chapter 15: Keeping Your Information Safe—
Contributing Author Doug Plass.............................................111

Conclusion...................................................................................123

About the Authors.......................................................................125

# Preface

In the Fall of 2017, I took on a case representing a client involved in a disability discrimination lawsuit. Although I had been practicing law for seventeen years at that point, I had only recently started my own law firm the year before. I was still the only attorney employed by my firm, and I was working out of my home office, spending most of my time counseling clients on how to comply with the law and how to stay out of court.

That being said, I came from a litigation background at my prior firm, so the prospect of adding some litigation work to the mix was exciting! This seemed like the perfect case for my firm to take on. I was sure I could handle it, and I could tell by reading the complaint that the case was defensible. By this time in my career, I was well-versed in the Americans with Disabilities Act, and I knew that the attorney who was representing the plaintiff did not specialize in employment law. Surely, my knowledge of the law would give me the edge I needed to win.

Of course, at that time, there was no way I could have known that this case would change the trajectory of my career. There was no way I could have known that it would take more than seven years to resolve that case.

There was no way I could have known that my firm would take that case all the way through a miserable two-week federal court trial. And there was no way I could have known that my client would spend hundreds of thousands of dollars over the course of that case in fees and costs.

My firm grew and morphed during the years that followed, and other attorneys came on board to assist with cases like this one. All told, six or seven attorneys at my firm worked on that case – sometimes it felt like (and still feels like) that case was going to go on forever. This is likely because the issues turned out to be more complicated than they initially seemed when we first took the case. Although we tried to get an early resolution of the case, the court declined. The case inched toward trial.

At some point, nearly a dozen employees of the agency I represented got deposed. The depositions were contentious, and the attorney on the other side, as is frequently the case with employment litigation, attacked each witness's ethics and integrity. Witnesses were accused of breaking the law and violating policy. Witnesses were accused of being liars. Witnesses were accused of being bad people overall. The depositions were stressful and uncomfortable. At one point, they were taking place in a conference room where the air conditioning stopped working. The witnesses, many of whom had never been deposed before, were drenched in sweat as they fought to maintain their composure. Inappropriate lines of questioning were pursued. I instructed the witnesses not to answer, and we got the judge on the phone to try to shut down the inappropriate line of questions. The witnesses were confused—they wondered why we were stopping the deposition to call the judge. As the case grew more and more contentious, and as my professional relationship with opposing counsel began to disintegrate, it felt like the deposition phase of the case would never end.

Fast forward to trial, which occurred two years later and after numerous attempts to settle the case had failed. The attorneys at my firm were ready. In a world where few civil cases actually make it to trial (less than

2%), we relished the chance to utilize our trial skills. The judge assigned to our case had a good reputation. We were excited to head into federal court to create some favorable law.

My client, on the other hand, was not excited. They recognized that having such a big trial, with numerous witnesses tied up, would sap the agency's productivity. Leadership recognized that an adverse outcome could have a detrimental effect on the agency's reputation. And, having experienced the discomfort of being deposed, some of the witnesses were scared and intimidated. They had seen enough of the attorney on the other side to realize he was bad news. Even more problematic, key witnesses felt bad for the plaintiff, who had brought the lawsuit after he was terminated. He had been their friend for many years, and they all lived in a relatively small community. It is an understatement to say they were uncomfortable testifying against him. We made a good-faith run at settlement, but it failed. The other side made unreasonable demands, and the decision was made to take the case to trial.

Ultimately, for everyone, trial was awful. It was stressful and uncomfortable, and at the end of each trial day, the witnesses were exhausted and disheartened. As it turns out, being a witness in a civil case is not fun and exciting. It definitely does not go down like it does on Netflix. Real-life courtroom experience is not glamorous, and it is not enjoyable. Witnesses are rarely able to outsmart the attorney who is cross-examining them.

The attorneys, myself included, did not fare much better than the witnesses. Between the weeks leading up to the trial and the trial itself, we had worked around the clock for nearly two months. It was exhausting and we did not see much of our families. Despite being well-prepared, we were caught off guard by the level of gameplay initiated by the attorneys on the other side. They did everything they could to distract the court from the true issues before it, and, as a result, we were frequently responding to ridiculous motions and issues that had little to do with the true facts of the case—all seemingly designed to divert us away from the merits of our case and to cost the client more time and money. By the end of the trial, we were stressed out. We were shell-shocked. We were disenchanted with the judicial process as a whole. We wished we had never gone to law school.

How did the trial end, you might be wondering? We lost. At the conclusion of the trial, the jury entered a verdict against my client. However, that was not the end of the story. About one year later, the court granted a mistrial, and the verdict, in its entirety, was set aside. Even today, as I write this book seven years after I first agreed to take on that case, parts of the case are still on appeal.

The case I described to you was not my first trial. However, it was the first trial I had ever participated in that was totally and completely miserable, and it was the first trial I had ever been a part of that made me question my career choice and our judicial process as a whole. I now view litigation work from a different lens. A trial may be necessary in some instances, and when that is the case, my firm still does trial work, and we do everything we can to help the employers we work with to maneuver through that process to obtain a successful outcome.

However, I now know, with 100 % certainty, that employers should do everything within their power to avoid claims and the court system at all costs. While employers cannot control some aspects impacting employment law liability, there is one aspect most employers can control: training. Employers can ensure that the leaders in their organization know the foundational basics needed to avoid employment law liability. They can ensure their supervisors, frequently the boots on the ground interacting with most employees in the workforce, are educated enough to flag issues before they create claims and liability. They can stay updated on the law to avoid silly mistakes that can land their business in trouble. That is the goal of this book: to arm employers with the knowledge and information they need to stay out of trouble.

# Introduction

It seems like a simple proposition: Every leader should have enough employment law training to know the basic issues that land employers in trouble. Every leader should have enough education to know how to avoid the most common mistakes. I am not suggesting that every leader needs a law degree. However, I am suggesting that every leader needs to know enough so they can spot issues that may lead to employment law liability. By this, I mean that every leader needs to recognize problematic issues so they can flag them for further analysis before they take an action that cannot be easily undone and that creates a claim or other liability.

Unfortunately, many leaders seem to resist this type of training. For some reason, many successful entrepreneurs and executive-level leadership types seem to believe that employment law concepts are so basic that they do not need any training on how to avoid pitfalls. They think that employment law is intuitive and that they can figure it out as they go. They are wrong.

Many of the issues that we will cover in this book are not intuitive, and unless a leader has experienced a similar situation before, it is unlikely that they would be able to successfully identify issues like these and unlikely that they would be able to make lawful decisions related to them unless they have some basic training.

Issues related to the Americans with Disabilities Act (ADA) are the easiest issues to point to that fall into this category. Many employers are surprised to hear that disability discrimination claims are one of the biggest sources of discrimination claims against employers, and oftentimes, there are more disability discrimination claims brought against employers in any given year than there are sexual harassment or gender discrimination claims. The reason for this is easy. The ADA was overhauled in 2008, and since that time, it has had an expansive reach and is intentionally very employee-friendly. Because the statutory scheme is relatively new, there continue to be new legal interpretations as to how an employer is required to respond in order to remain compliant. For example, unless an employer knows that mental health disabilities are covered under the ADA, and unless an employer has a general idea of what that means and how to proceed in response to that, an employer may make a decision that triggers liability under the ADA without even knowing or understanding that the ADA was implicated in the first place.

Issues related to drug and alcohol use in the workplace are another example of areas ripe for mistakes by employers. There is nothing intuitive about how an employer should respond to a complaint that a recovering alcoholic is drinking on the job. And there is nothing intuitive as to how an employer should respond to a belief brought forward by a manager that an employee who recently had surgery is under the influence of opioids in the workplace. These areas are covered by the ADA and require some basic knowledge and training. No matter how sophisticated or intelligent a leader may be, they simply cannot guess their way through these types of issues without expecting to incur potential liability.

Another reason employers sometimes fail to get training is because they expect their Human Resource (HR) professionals to handle all aspects of employment law that may touch upon their workplace. This is an unrealistic view. While an organization's HR professionals may well be the point people for the analysis and resolution of employment law problems and issues, they simply cannot be expected to be the only ones flagging every potential employment law issue that arises. This is especially true when a business has supervisors who maintain most of the day-to-day contact within the company.

For example, imagine a business with one hundred employees that has an HR Director and several supervisors who manage different departments. Most likely, on any given day, the supervisors interact more with the employees than the HR director. And, on any given day, if the supervisors do not recognize that information they are receiving or perceiving relates to an employment law issue, they may make a decision that creates a claim before HR is even made aware that the problem exists. This is why training is so important—every leader within an organization needs to know enough to avoid problems, and if an employer shifts that burden to one person, it is unlikely that the employer will succeed in avoiding claims and litigation.

By reading this book, you have taken the first step in being well on your way to avoiding problems and liability. Nicely done! But wait—there is more good news. The list of topics you need to know to get a basic sense of the key issues that land employers in trouble is somewhat limited. I can say that over the course of my twenty-four years of practicing law, I typically see the same issues over and over again, resulting in claims and lawsuits against employers. That has resulted in my team's ability to write a somewhat short and concise list of topics in this book. These are the frequent fliers, so to speak, of the types of issues that keep the doors of my law firm open because they happen over and over again, and if an organization fails to take basic steps to ensure its leaders know some basic concepts, they may well draw a claim in this area. The idea behind this book is simple: If you familiarize yourself with these concepts, and if you know enough to flag a problem when it comes up, you can hopefully stay out of the courthouse altogether.

We have now come to the point in this book where a few disclaimers are in order. One relates to one of my favorite things about employment law, which led me to focus my career on this practice area—the fact that the law is always changing. In fact, as social norms change, and even as politics and political administrations change, the same holds true with the law in this area. This means that leaders need to pay attention to the law and get updated training over time. So, while you are to be congratulated for picking up this book and taking some easy steps to staying out of the courthouse, you should know that over the course of your career, you may need updated training, and there may be new areas that pop up that require some time and attention on your part. Be on the lookout for those and consider getting some type of refresher on a yearly basis. Be aware that the law could have changed since the date this book was published.

You should also know that this book focuses on some general federal employment law concepts that largely apply throughout the United States. However, state law is not covered in this book, and many states have more detailed laws and regulations than what will be covered in this book. This means that while the concepts here are very important, there may be other important state and local laws layered on top of the ones that you will learn about here. How will you know? Talking to local employment law counsel licensed in your state is one easy way to ensure you are compliant in all aspects of employment law.

So, dive in and see what you think. Some issues might speak more loudly to you than others (although I would be surprised if you already know and understand all of the basic concepts applicable under the ADA). If you find an issue that resonates, you will now be armed with enough information to grow and learn how to follow the law in order to avoid problems. Feel free to use my book to help your organization change and grow. Maybe that means implementing new policies and protocols or updating your handbook. Maybe that means lobbying for company-wide training. Maybe that means opening the lines of communication in the discipline or termination process. At any rate, you now have some tools to guide you.

CHAPTER 1

# Why Supervisors Need More Training and What That Training Looks Like

You might be wondering why you need to have training on key employment law principles. The answer is easy—supervisors are held to a higher standard. In other words, if a former employee claims that a supervisor harassed them, it will be difficult for the employer to defend the lawsuit. If you manage people, the law assumes that your employer has given you the education, knowledge, and tools to do this.

There is a case that the US Supreme Court decided several years back. It involved a female food service worker who claimed her supervisor was harassing her based on her race. The employer defended itself by arguing that the woman accused of harassment was not a supervisor. The whole case hinged on whether the woman was a supervisor or not. WHY? Because under the law, supervisors are held to a higher standard. This makes it easier for an employee to argue that they have been harassed or discriminated against. If the supervisor is the one accused of unlawful conduct, it is easier under the law for the employee to prevail.

But even setting all of that aside, in order for a supervisor to fulfill the role they have been put in—managing others—they need to know how to supervise and what the job encompasses. I can't tell you all of those things, and it does differ for every employer. But what I can share with you are some basic concepts that lead to employment law liability that universally apply to all supervisors.

We've just covered one—the law imposes a higher standard on supervisors. Another one is this: Supervisors need to know what policies their employers have put in place, and they need to know what the expectations are from their employer regarding how to enforce the policies.

Look at the handbook. No, it's not exciting, but those are the policies that set the ground rules for your workplace. If an employee does not follow the policy, your supervisors need to know what to do. Should they verbally coach them, should they draft a memo to the file, or should they do a written warning? Those are all good questions for your workplace to resolve before a question or a problem arises.

Who do you address those questions to? Is it HR? Is it a higher-level supervisor? Again, these are great questions to ask to make sure everyone in the decision-making chain is looped in.

One last comment on why supervisors should have training. If you do end up with a claim or a lawsuit, just by showing you received and/ or provided training, your company stands a better chance of putting forward a viable defense. That is certainly not the only reason you would want to have training and to know and understand the law, but it is a good one. Think about it: If you are accused of breaking the law, wouldn't you want to be able to argue that you made every effort to know and follow the law? Hopefully, the answer is yes, and that is what we are trying to assist with here.

# CHAPTER 2

# What Does it Mean to Be an At-Will Employee and Why You Need to Know the Answer to That Question

Sometimes, I get asked by employers, "Since we live in an at-will employment state, can't we just fire employees for any reason?" The answer to that question is that you can fire employees in an at-will state. However, if you are not able to show that you did so for a legitimate reason, you might get sued for discrimination, and you might have a hard time putting forward a solid defense.

Not every state follows concepts of at-will employment, so make sure you understand whether the state or states you are operating in follows this doctrine. The concept of at-will employment essentially means that an employer is free to terminate an employee for any reason or no reason, at any time, as long as the reason they are terminating the employee is lawful.

Take my client, Sue, for example. Sue got fed up with her long-time employee, Teri, because Teri seemed disengaged and had developed a bad attitude. Sue heard from others that Teri was telling everyone Sue was a bad manager, and this was upsetting to Sue. Sue ultimately decided that it would be easier to fire Teri than to have a lengthy performance discussion with her. So, one day, when Teri was walking around making snide comments to her co-workers, Sue pulled the trigger on her termination. One week later, Sue received a demand letter from a local law firm that represents plaintiffs (in this case, employees seeking to sue employers). Teri's lawyer cited a recent birthday card that Sue had given to Teri, wishing her a happy birthday and wishing her much success in her new decade of life. Her lawyer claimed that obviously Sue was thinking about Teri's age and had decided to clean house on older members of the workforce.

The attorney told Sue that in Teri's twenty years of service to the company, the company had never disciplined Teri or told her she was doing anything wrong. And this, the attorney believed, showed that any claim on the part of the company that Teri was fired for performance issues was false. The attorney gave Sue an option: write a big check or spend the next few years in a contentious lawsuit.

In order to understand where Sue went wrong, it is important to understand the basic concept of at-will employment. Again, this means that an employer can fire an employee for any reason or no reason as long as it's for a lawful reason. So what does that mean to you as a supervisor if you live in an at-will employment state? It means that even if you live in an at-will state, you need to be able to show if you discipline or terminate an employee (or otherwise adversely impact an employee's terms or conditions of employment), that you did so for lawful and legal reasons.

Why does that matter? Because even in states that follow the at-will employment doctrine, employers still get sued all of the time for discrimination and harassment. Employees bring lawsuits arguing that they were treated unlawfully or illegally, creating a need for you to be able to show that what you are doing, you are doing for lawful, legitimate, and legal reasons. You do this by taking the time before you ever terminate someone to think through whether you can show you are doing it for a lawful reason. In lawyer speak, we sometimes call this being able to prove that the employer did what they did for legitimate, non-discriminatory reasons.

The primary way you do this is by reviewing your documentation and preparing appropriate documentation if you don't have any. If you are terminating an employee for a performance problem, do you have it documented somewhere that you told the employee about the performance problem and gave them a chance to fix it? That is the best documentation—a document created at the time the problem arose that shows you acted fairly. Ideally, when you terminate an employee, you will have documentation showing that you told the employee about the problem, you gave them a chance to fix it, and the employee failed to do so.

There is no one-size-fits-all as to what the documentation needs to look like. You might have the performance issue or policy violation documented in an end-of-year review, a coaching email, or a written warning, but it is very important that if you are going to terminate someone for a performance issue that you have it documented somewhere that the problem was identified and discussed with the employee. At the heart of most employment law discrimination lawsuits is a lack of documentation and a basic understanding of the concept of at-will employment is needed in order to create the documentation you need.

**CHAPTER 3**

# Why You Need to Document Performance Issues and What Your Documentation Needs to Say

If you don't document a performance issue, it's tough to prove that an employee had a performance problem. Again, as we have already covered, every time a supervisor takes disciplinary action, they should be able to show they did what they did for legitimate, legal reasons. And, if a manager or a supervisor does not document performance issues that eventually support disciplinary action, it opens the door for an employee to argue that they were a great performer and that there were no disciplinary problems. In fact, in nearly every claim and lawsuit my firm defends, the employee argues they were a stellar performer and that there was no basis for the employer to discipline and/or terminate them. In nearly every discrimination case, the employee then uses this argument to support the conclusion that the employer must have disciplined them for some illegal reason—like protected class status—instead of for a legitimate performance issue.

Without documentation to back up the supervisor's perspective, if a lawsuit follows, it turns into a "he-said, she-said" situation. It is the manager's word against the employee's word, and sometimes, the employee comes across to a jury as being more believable. As a litigator, I want the employers I work with to have documentation so we can easily prove that they did what they did for legitimate reasons. This type of documentation undoubtedly becomes some of the most important evidence there is in a trial. If documentation like this exists, in most cases, the employer will be able to establish a solid defense for most types of discrimination claims.

I have heard many reasons as to why a supervisor does not want to document a performance issue. "I don't put things down because I don't want the people who report to me not to like me." Or, "I would rather coach them off the record than put something in writing that could harm their career." Or, "If I spent all of my time drafting written warnings, I would not have any time to actually supervise my crew."

There is merit to these concerns. I would never advise a supervisor that they should spend all of their time trying to get the employees who report to them in trouble, and I would never tell a supervisor that every deficiency they observe should end up in a formal write-up. I agree that if every supervisor managed their employees that way, they would be ineffective and unlikeable.

What I would say, instead, is this: There are many ways to help coach your employees so they are aware of the things they are not doing well and the things they are doing well. If a supervisor views their role as one where they are doing more coaching than disciplining, then it opens up a number of possibilities as to the best way to do both things: make sure employees know what they are not doing right and that this is documented. In other words, a good supervisor will let their employees know if they are not meeting expectations and how they can improve their performance so they are meeting expectations. Along these same lines, a good supervisor will make sure the employees at issue are crystal clear on exactly what those expectations are. There are many, many ways a supervisor can put this in writing, so if the issue later blows up, the supervisor has documentation to show that a performance issue did, in fact, exist.

One of the easiest ways to do this is through an email. If a supervisor has a coaching session, they could simply send themselves an email for the file that shows they coached an employee for a potential performance problem and that describes the substance of that conversation. Boom. That alone is simple enough, but it would also get the job done. What if a supervisor does not have email? It doesn't matter! They could scratch out some notes on a notepad and send that to HR to keep in a file. As long as someone can read it and understand it, this, too, would get the job done. The format does not matter. It is the language contained within it that is key. Other ways to do this include the traditional means: written warnings, performance improvement plans, and evaluations or reviews.

The only thing worse than no documentation, however, is bad documentation. There are several things that can turn documentation into evidence that can be used against you if a problem arises, and employers need to make sure some basic documentation guidelines are followed.

First, honesty is important. Documentation that says an employee is performing well when the employee is performing badly is a problem. We defended a case not long ago where an employer fired an employee for severe performance issues. Unfortunately, one month before the termination, the employer gave the employee a stellar performance review. Unsurprisingly, the employee retained a lawyer who argued that the employee was not fired for performance issues but rather because the employer discriminated against people with disabilities. The lesson here is that if the employer does not have a good grasp on how the employee is performing, or if the supervisor is not good at delivering difficult messages, they should not be the one to give the employee a review. And they certainly should not give them a glowing review.

Sometimes, the problem lies with a supervisor who is unwilling to have a difficult performance conversation with an employee. If a supervisor is not able to convey truthful performance criticisms in the documentation they create, then someone else should assist the supervisor in drafting and presenting the review. Many a lawsuit was premised on a performance review saying that the employee was performing well when, in reality, the employee was not.

In addition to honesty, timing is important. Documentation created to identify and/or discuss a performance problem should be created when the problem occurs, not many months later. If documentation is created long after the problem arises, it is suspect and opens the door for an employee to question the accuracy of (and the motive behind) the document.

Also important is the language that goes into the documentation. Supervisors or others who create documentation need to know and understand why they should avoid any mention of or reference to protected class information.

On the other hand, specific facts and details should be included to avoid any confusion or ambiguity as to what the real problem is. Dates of performance problems, the policies or performance expectations that have been violated, and how they were violated would all be the type of facts to include. Why? Because vague and ambiguous performance documents open the door for mischief. Take this example: Imagine a supervisor who attempts to create a performance improvement plan related to a sales employee who is not meeting the quota for the required number of sales calls per day. The supervisor creates a document that says things like, "Performance is inadequate." However, the supervisor does not describe how and does not give the dates the performance fell short.

Several months later, the employer terminates the employee because the performance did not improve. The employee then brings a claim under the Pregnant Workers Fairness Act, claiming that she had been on parental leave for part of the year, and she believes that the supervisor's comments in the document were criticisms of her absence during the time she took advantage of the employer's parental leave program. The employee argues that the employer does not like it when employees request accommodations during pregnancy and that the employer looks for ways to terminate women who are of childbearing age.

If the supervisor had included specific dates that the employee's performance fell short and specifically mentioned policy violations and shortcomings related to her failure to meet the sales quota when she was not pregnant, the employee's argument would likely have failed. However, when a supervisor includes vague and ambiguous criticisms that can neither be proved nor disproven, the documentation can be more of a hindrance than a help.

### *Here are some tips when considering documentation:*

- Documentation can come in many forms, including notes from conversations, counseling emails, performance improvement plans, written warnings, and notes.

- Documentation is not always a negative thing. It opens the pathway for clear communication and can help an employee recognize and improve a problem.

- Include detailed facts about the basis for discipline, with dates.

- If applicable, cite policies that address the relevant issues, standards, quotas, and goals.

- Describe what will happen if conduct does not improve.

- Give dates by which improvement needs to be seen.

- Require the employee's signature.

- Don't use vague and ambiguous statements or mention any protected class status.

- Documentation should be created contemporaneously as problems arise.

- Include specific steps the employee should take to improve.

## CHAPTER 4

# Discipline and Termination

Imagine this scenario. Stephanie wanted to terminate her long-time bookkeeper, Stacy, who was from South Korea. Stacy's performance had never quite met Stephanie's expectations, and one month, when cash flow was bad, Stephanie decided to terminate her. Notably, Stephanie had not documented how or when Stacy had failed to meet her expectations. And, at the time Stephanie moved forward with the termination, Stacy's personnel file only contained positive performance comments like an annual review performed six months earlier that said Stacy was an asset to the company.

Stacy was blindsided and upset by the termination. Several weeks after she was let go, she hired a lawyer and accused Stephanie of racial and national origin discrimination. Stacy's lawyer argued that she was a great performer (as evidenced by her personnel file, which was void of negative performance indicators). He argued that the real reason Stacy was fired was because of her race and national origin, not her performance. He cited the fact that every other member of Stephanie's leadership team was white and stated Stacy's belief that she was being fired because she did not fit the company profile, not because of her performance.

If Stephanie had only paused the termination process long enough to set aside emotion and to analyze risk, she likely would not have gone through with the termination, as she would have realized that Stacy's race and national origin, coupled with the lack of documentation as to her performance problems, created a dangerous situation for her. It wasn't that Stephanie needed to keep Stacy employed indefinitely. However, in order to guard against the racial discrimination claim that ended up being made against her, Stephanie should have paused the process long enough to analyze risk factors and to get some documentation in the file concerning Stacy's performance issues.

This is one example of why we recommend that any time an employer is terminating or disciplining an employee, they should run through a checklist to determine how much risk there is with going forward and whether there are steps that need to occur before the termination happens. Checklists are a handy tool—you don't need to memorize the various risk factors that can lead to a claim, but you should always have a tool available that can remind you of what those factors might be. As we all know, discipline and termination conversations and decisions can be emotional and difficult. It is better to head into such a situation armed with a basic analysis of why your decision is solid, and if you do this, your odds of drawing a claim go down.

What should be on the checklist, you may be wondering? There is no one-size-fits-all that covers every issue you should analyze. However, it would not be a bad idea to use a checklist tailored to specific issues in your state.

One preliminary issue to cover is whether the employee at issue is a party to an employment agreement. Is the employee at-will, or is there some specific time period of employment? Can the employee be terminated for any legal reason, or is there a legal document indicating that the employee can only be terminated for certain reasons? These are basic questions that need to be answered on the front end.

Likewise, does the employer's handbook or other policies create a need for an employer to give notice or to perform some other task before termination occurs? Some employers build in due-process-type protocols aimed at ensuring fairness. For those employers, it is important that their supervisors and other leaders with authority to terminate recognize those requirements and ensure they are followed before and during termination.

Protected class status is another area that creates risk with termination or discipline. Your checklist should ask questions like, "Is the employee at issue over forty? Are they a member of a race that is non-Caucasian? Are they from a country other than the United States? Are they a woman, or are they LGBTQ+? Are they pregnant?" These same questions should be asked in regard to military status and religion, as membership to any protected class can flag a need for additional analysis before discipline or termination occurs.

Medical issues, disabilities, and issues related to disabilities can also create risk, and these questions reserve an important spot on the checklist. Anytime you have an employee who is working through the ADA accommodation process, it signals a need to slow down and analyze the situation before moving forward. This also holds true for situations involving an employee who has requested or taken Family and Medical Leave Act (FMLA) leave or who has suffered an injury covered by worker's compensation. Will you be able to show that you are terminating the employee for a lawful reason? Or are there facts that would enable an employee to argue that they are being terminated because of a disability, a medical condition, or their exercise of legal rights?

Sometimes, employers overlook how important it can be to give long-time employees special consideration. If your business has kept an employee on your payroll for several decades, one could draw the assumption that the employee was a good performer. Take the example of Stacy above. Certainly, in the case brought against Stephanie's company, Stacy's lawyer will cite the fact that Stacy was employed for many years and did not have any record of prior discipline. For long-time employees, an employer always needs to be able to show that something has changed that has created the need for the employer to move forward with termination. This is where well-drafted and timely documentation comes into play. A counseling document showing that the employee is not meeting performance expectations could have made all of the difference in the defense of Stacy's lawsuit. In many instances, the documentation is easy to create and place in the employee's personnel file. However, a failure to recognize the need for such documentation can be detrimental.

One area on the checklist that is sometimes overlooked is whether or not the employee has engaged in protected activity. There are many types of whistleblowing claims out there, both in the private and public sectors, and most of them boil down to whether or not an employee can cite facts that indicate they engaged in some type of protected activity and then were terminated or disciplined as a result of that activity.

Take Title VII, the federal statute that prevents many types of discrimination based on protected class status. Title VII has anti-retaliation provisions that provide protection for an employee who brings a complaint of discrimination or harassment forward or who participates in an investigation related to a claim. If an employee were to bring a claim of harassment to her supervisor or an HR representative, then that employee has engaged in protected activity that warrants additional consideration before a disciplinary or termination decision is made. If an employer fails to recognize the risk and moves forward with termination on the heels of a harassment report, the employee could bring a retaliation claim and argue that the real reason they were terminated was because they brought a complaint forward and not because of any performance issues.

While participation in an investigation is one type of protected activity, there are other types of conduct that could fall into that bucket, as well. For example, take a situation where an employee brings a wage and hour compliance issue forward, indicating to the employer that the company may be in violation of the law. If the employee is terminated the next week, it could give an appearance that the employee was fired because they raised concerns about legal violations, another type of protected activity. Or imagine if you fire an employee who raised a safety concern to the Occupational Safety and Health Administration (OSHA)? Or an employee who was cooperating with the Department of Labor in regard to an audit or investigation? All of those scenarios could create risk with a termination.

Going through the items in a checklist may take some time, and, as you may now recognize, it might create a need for the person contemplating discipline or termination to coordinate with other leaders in your organization in order to obtain answers to the facts at issue.

In fact, fairness and uniformity among leaders when it comes to discipline and termination decisions is another important factor to consider. Sometimes, employers forget to consider whether policies are being uniformly enforced, and that, too, can create a risk. What if one supervisor, perhaps one in charge of a group of Hispanic women over forty, aggressively disciplines for performance shortfalls while another supervisor, who just happens to supervise a group of white men mostly under forty, does not? This is the type of uneven policy enforcement that can lead to problems, as it opens the door for the Hispanic women to argue that they are being disciplined not because of performance problems but rather because Hispanic women over forty are held to a higher standard because of their protected class status. An employer can avoid this by ensuring that supervisors are communicating or, alternatively, through a mechanism by which someone like HR can ensure that the type of discipline or termination at issue is consistently being enforced.

In one recent case in which we were involved, the employer did not go through the checklist. Thus, the high-level leader who pulled the trigger on the termination had no idea that the employee she fired was on FMLA leave, had a disability accommodation, and had just reported a wage and hour violation to company leaders. When a leader moves forward without thinking through the risk and without involving others who would have answers to the questions on the checklist, it can result in years of protracted litigation and high settlement costs. A checklist can avoid all of that.

### Considerations to keep in mind for discipline and termination:

- Be careful of relying on at-will employment and declining to give a basis for termination.

- Cite policy violations or standards/quotas/objectives that were not met, if applicable.

- Run through the checklist to assess risk before moving forward with discipline or termination.

- Consult with HR and other leaders who would have information about potential areas of risk before moving forward with termination.

- Avoid discipline or termination based on emotion.

- If documentation does not exist to support legitimate, non-discriminatory reasons for termination, consider slowing the process down to get documentation in place.

- Beware of terminating long-time employees for poor performance.

- Beware of terminating employees for performance who have recently received a favorable review.

- Consider severance if a high-risk employee is at issue.

- Bring in legal counsel to weigh in on risk if necessary.

## CHAPTER 5

# Why Continual Training on Discrimination and Harassment is Needed

You might be thinking, *I have had sexual harassment training, so I don't need any other training on this.* Even if you have had training in the past, supervisors should be receiving continually updated training. Why? Because the law on harassment and discrimination is broader than sexual harassment and because the law is constantly changing. Our discussion is going to focus on the federal laws that prohibit discrimination, including Title VII, the ADA, and the Age Discrimination in Employment Act (ADEA). However, there could be state laws where you live that create additional liability for you to be aware of, too.

Let's talk about how the law has changed and evolved. Take, for example, the laws that prohibit discrimination on the basis of sex. This law is not new. In fact, it dates back over fifty years to when Title VII first rolled out as part of the Civil Rights movement. What has changed is the interpretation of the word "sex." In fact, I think we can all agree that social norms have changed and evolved in many, many areas since the 1960's when the Civil Rights Act went into effect.

Most recently, in 2020, the United States Supreme Court conclusively determined that gender identity and sexual orientation are encompassed within the word "sex," as it is used in Title VII. In other words, while there was a significant period of time where discrimination on the basis of sex referred to female employees, that no longer holds true, and discrimination on the basis of sex includes members of the LGBTQ+ class, females, and pregnant women, as well. This is one reason why continual training for leaders is a must: Social norms change, laws change, and the concepts related to the law change and morph over time, too.

Changing technology falls into this bucket, as well. Think of how members of your workplace now communicate.

- Do they use a chat function or send direct messages via third-party platforms?

- Do they communicate on social media?

- Does your workplace utilize remote workers?

- Is AI a part of your workplace and how your employees communicate?

All of these concepts continue to change and develop, and the way in which they could give rise to discrimination and/or harassment claims will only continue to change and grow. This is one more reason that updated training is needed.

CHAPTER 6

# Workplace Discrimination and Harassment—Contributing Author Jennifer M. Walrath

## *Is It Discrimination?*

Layla and Marcie are nail technicians at a hotel spa. Both of them are originally from Guatemala, and sometimes, they speak Spanish to each other at work. Their workstations are next to one another, and one day, while each of them is giving a manicure to a customer, they begin speaking in Spanish about one of the customers, including negative comments about the customer. As it turns out, the customer speaks Spanish, too, understands what they are saying, and is upset. The spa manager does not like that Layla and Marcie upset the customer and decides that the obvious solution is to prohibit them from speaking Spanish at work.

Another employee at the hotel spa, Adrian, works as a masseuse. Adrian was born a male but identifies as female, presents as female, and asks that co-workers use she/her pronouns when referring to her at work. Adrian is black and prefers to keep her hair in long, tight braids, partly because she believes it makes her look more feminine but also because it is an easier way to maintain her hair. One of Adrian's customers complains that Adrian's hair kept brushing against her during the massage, but also compliments the fact that Adrian had such strong hands for a female masseuse. One of Adrian's co-workers jumps into the conversation and says, "Well, that's because Adrian is a man pretending to be a woman," which upsets the customer, who had requested a female masseuse.

The spa manager wants to discipline Adrian for violating the spa's dress code and grooming policy, which requires all personnel to maintain their hair in a way that does not interfere with their work. The manager also does not want another situation where a customer who requested a female masseuse becomes upset if/when they learn Adrian biologically is a man, so the manager instructs staff who assign masseuses not to assign Adrian to any customer who specifically requests a female masseuse. Adrian's compensation is based, in part, on how many customers she provides services to, and after this rule is put in place, Adrian starts to see a decline in the number of customers assigned to her and a decline in her pay.

Would your supervisors and managers be able to recognize that there are issues of possible discrimination under Title VII of the Civil Rights Act of 1964? Would your supervisors and managers know enough to hit pause on these disciplinary decisions and seek input on what to do and whether what they are considering is appropriate under the law?

Title VII prohibits discrimination based on race, color, national origin, religion, and sex. Other federal laws also prohibit discrimination based on age and disability. Age-based discrimination is prohibited by the ADEA, and disability-based discrimination is prohibited by the ADA. All of these laws make it illegal to treat someone differently or unfavorably because of the person's protected class status, including when it comes to hiring, firing, compensation, job assignments, benefits, and any other term or condition of employment.

This does not mean that employers cannot have conduct- and performance-based expectations for their employees. What is important is to have policies and expectations that are generally applicable and uniformly applied to all similarly situated employees. It is also critical that disciplinary, pay-related, and other decisions that impact an employee at work are made with an eye toward whether and how the decision could relate to an employee's protected class status and whether it could raise issues under the law.

Going back to our spa manager and Layla and Marcie, who offended a customer by saying negative things about her in Spanish, the manager can take action to address the situation. However, the manager must be careful not to discriminate against Layla and Marcie based on their national origin, which includes spoken languages. Policies that restrict employees' ability to speak languages other than English are discriminatory and violate Title VII if they are put in place due to bias against employees of a particular national origin. English-only policies that apply at all times, even while employees are on breaks, tend to show that a policy is discriminatory. By contrast, English-only policies that apply in certain limited situations and exist for substantial and legitimate business reasons can be permissible.

For our spa manager, the real concern is not so much that Layla and Marcie were speaking Spanish but that they were making negative comments about a customer in front of the customer. Layla and Marcie could be disciplined for insulting a customer, which was not acceptable employee behavior, irrespective of the language spoken. The spa also may consider requiring that all employees speak a common language (English) during those times when they are providing services to customers, though the spa should give thorough consideration to its client base, whether customers predominantly speak English or some other language, and whether there truly is a business necessity that customer-facing staff speak only English.

Our spa manager also made a misstep in addressing the situation involving Adrian. Ever since the U.S. Supreme Court's 2020 decision in *Bostock v. Clayton County*, it has been clear that the protections under Title VII on the basis of "sex" extend to gender identity and sexual orientation. Adrian's gender identity affords her protected class status, and the spa manager's decision not to let Adrian work with customers who request female masseuses adversely impacted Adrian's compensation, which is a term of employment. If Adrian chose to bring a claim against the spa for discrimination based on sex, she likely would have a valid claim, and chances are good that she would be able to prevail.

By contrast, it was acceptable for the manager to discipline Adrian for violations of the spa's dress code and grooming policy. The policy is written in a way that is uniform and generally applicable, and Adrian does not need to alter her hairstyle to comply but should simply restrain her hair in some fashion (e.g., bun or ponytail) while working. Such a requirement is consistent with the needs of the business, and any employee who has long hair, regardless of hair texture or particular hairstyle, would have to comply.

Employers have to be careful that their grooming policies are not discriminatory, for example, by prohibiting men from having long hair while allowing it for women or by directly or indirectly prohibiting certain hair styles associated with certain races or ethnicities. Employers also should be aware that some U.S. states have CROWN Acts, which expressly forbid hair-based discrimination in the workplace and may have additional requirements beyond Title VII.

In the case of our spa manager, even though disciplining Adrian for violating the spa's grooming policy ended up being all right, it is not clear that the manager thought through the race-based issues implicated by the situation before deciding to take that action. Before taking any disciplinary action, it is advisable to think through whether there are any potential issues related to protected class status under Title VII, the

ADEA, the ADA, or state law. Not all supervisors and business leaders know enough about the law to be able to do this, and not all high-level leaders know enough about legal risk and potential fall-out when things go wrong to take it seriously and get the right policies, procedures, and training in place.

## Is It Harassment?

Going back to our hotel spa, Adrian is having issues with one of her co-workers, James. James is a devout Catholic and does not believe that someone can have a gender identity different from how they were born. James refuses to use Adrian's preferred pronouns (she/her) and often uses the terms "man" or "dude" when referring to Adrian. James also comments on Adrian's attire, saying that he does not think it is appropriate for Adrian to wear skirts, and that he finds it odd that Adrian has painted fingernails. Adrian tells the spa manager about James' conduct toward her and reports that she finds it offensive. Adrian asks the spa manager to tell James to stop making these kinds of comments and asks that the manager tell James to use Adrian's preferred pronouns and stop misgendering Adrian. The manager talks to James, who says that everything he has said or done is because of his religious beliefs, which are really important to him. The manager does not really know what to do, so he just tells James to try to be nicer to Adrian.

Meanwhile, James is open about his religious beliefs at work and talks often about his Catholic faith and plans to attend bible studies or go to mass. Chad, the owner of the spa, is agnostic and believes that people who subscribe to "traditional religion" are being misled and their human spirits suffocated. Whenever Chad sees James at work, he asks probing questions about James' faith, insinuates that James is foolish for buying into what the Catholic church tells him, and conveys his "strong hope" that James will wake up one day and free himself from the shackles of organized religion. Many spa employees agree with Chad that "traditional" organized religions, like Catholicism, are antiquated, prejudiced, and not in step with mainstream society. Although Chad says that he would never require employees to agree with him or abandon their religious beliefs, he often makes comments when he visits the spa about how James does not really fit in at work, and Chad has asked the spa manager to keep track of how often James talks about his faith at work. James remains committed to his faith, but he feels like he has to limit how much he talks about it and that he has to pretend to have some skepticism about his religion, or else he will be ostracized or possibly even terminated.

Would your high-level leaders realize that these are instances of possible harassment? That an employee can be harassed based on their gender identity, and that even religious beliefs may not excuse such harassing conduct? That ostracizing an employee because of his religious beliefs can be harassment based on religion in violation of Title VII?

Harassment is a form of discrimination that is prohibited under the law. Collectively, Title VII, the ADA, and the ADEA prohibit harassment on the basis of race, color, national origin, religion, sex, disability, and age. Harassment can come in many forms. Often, it is in the form of a hostile work environment created by offensive conduct over a period of time. The conduct must be both subjectively offensive to the employee, in that it is unwelcome, and objectively offensive in that a reasonable person would find it hostile or abusive.

The conduct also must be sufficiently severe or pervasive so as to impact the terms and conditions of employment. The more severe the conduct, the less pervasive it needs to be, and a serious single incident (e.g., sexual assault) can be harassment. The less severe the conduct, the more pervasive it must be in order to constitute harassment. For example, things like jokes, derogatory or lewd comments, or innuendos, if made with enough frequency over a period of time, can have a cumulative effect that is harassing.

Harassment also can come in the form of favoritism toward employees who go along with harassing behavior or adverse employment actions (e.g., denial of promotion or pay raise) against employees who refuse to allow or refuse to overlook harassing conduct. A common example when it comes to sexual harassment is the young female employee who refuses to go on a date with her male supervisor and finds herself demoted or routinely overlooked for advancement opportunities even though she is one of the most qualified candidates.

Returning to our hotel spa, both Adrian and James potentially are being subjected to unlawful harassment—Adrian on the basis of her gender identity and James on the basis of his religion. There are a lot of complicated questions when it comes to balancing an employer's obligations to protect employees from harassment with the rights of free speech and religious expression, and we will not be digging into those complex issues here. It is important, however, to be confident that your business leaders can recognize that situations like these raise issues of potential harassment and that, unlike our spa manager, they have some idea of what to do—even if the "what to do" is not an immediate solution, but to escalate it appropriately and involve someone else in trying to work through the issue.

A leader who is not educated enough about the law will not be able to do this. Training is critical. Also, because issues of discrimination and harassment tend to evolve with the times and social norms, older training is likely to be outdated and unhelpful—even harmful. For example, until more recently, employers did not have to grapple with issues of gender identity as they do now. It was only four years ago that the U.S. Supreme Court recognized gender identity as protected under Title VII. Even more recently, in 2024, the Equal Employment Opportunity Commission (EEOC), which enforces Title VII, issued updated anti-harassment guidance that makes clear that preventing harassment and discrimination on the basis of gender identity is a primary policy objective. It is an important and ever-evolving issue, and it is not going away. Business leaders need to be aware of and understand it, which is where training—specifically modern updated training—comes in.

## Is That All?

Not by a long shot! This is a vast area of the law that covers a lot of issues and topics, and that covers a lot of employees in any given workplace. There is a lot that is not covered here, but if you keep the following top takeaways in mind and act on them, you will be well on your way to having your house in order:

- Have a robust anti-harassment and anti-discrimination policy and make sure that it is up to date to address recent changes in the law.

- Train all employees on your anti-harassment and anti-discrimination policy and do it regularly! We recommend training annually.

- Provide additional, more in-depth training for your supervisors, HR professionals, and business leaders. This is critically important! Supervisors (and business owners) are held to higher standards when it comes to anti-harassment in particular, and they are expected to know the law and what not to do.

- Keep up to date on trends and changes in the law. This is an area where changes in social norms can have a significant impact both on the law itself and on the nature of the issues that tend to come up in the workplace.

- Know when to get help! Some of these issues are complicated, especially if they involve competing protected interests among employees, and being able to recognize the need to get help is half the battle.

CHAPTER 7

# What to Do When a Report Comes In

Our client Steve was lucky. His company, which was large and successful, had never had to deal with a harassment or discrimination complaint. But several weeks ago, a female employee, Cheryl, walked into his office and told him that she was being sexually harassed. Steve was upset. He believed Cheryl, but he could not imagine that the supervisor at issue would be so stupid as to do the things that Cheryl said he did. He wanted the issue resolved immediately, but he had no idea how to proceed. Steve was smart and had received enough training to know that complaints need to be handled quickly and appropriately. He called us in order to figure out an approach to handling the complaint that would both comply with the law and reduce his company's risk and liability. Steve knew that no one in his workplace was trained to handle investigations like this one.

As a result, we hired a third-party workplace investigator to help his company gather facts and analyze any information related to the issue of whether Cheryl had been harassed. When the investigator had issued her written report, we helped Steve assess the situation. Based on the investigative report and prior disciplinary issues related to the supervisor at issue, Steve ultimately terminated the supervisor. We counseled him through the various communications that needed to take place. And then, we helped line up anti-harassment training for his office. Steve's issue was resolved without further incident.

Not all leaders identify this issue with the level of importance that should be associated with it. Sometimes clients try to handle the issue on their own and attempt to undertake an internal investigation to figure out what happened. Take a former client, Dana, for example. Dana's company received a complaint that Scott had sexually harassed his subordinate, James. Dana ran the company and decided to handle the situation herself. After talking to James, she made the decision that Scott, who was openly gay, was a harasser and fired him. She did not document the discussion, nor did she write an investigative report. She did not review her company's internal policy on harassment and discrimination and did not follow the guidance within it. Even worse, she did not even talk to Scott to get his side of the story. She had no prior training or experience in conducting an investigation, and yet she conducted the investigation herself (sort of) and did not call legal counsel or her outside HR consultant for help.

About a month after terminating Scott, Dana's company received an EEOC complaint from Scott, claiming the company discriminated against him on the basis of his gender. When Scott was given a chance to tell his side of the story, he explained that James had made sexual advances toward him, and when he declined the offer, James was upset and concocted the story about Scott harassing him.

When an employer receives a complaint of harassment or discrimination, it is essential that they act quickly and appropriately. As holds true for most employment law issues, there is not one set path that applies to any and all situations. Instead, the approach varies based on a number of different issues, including the nature of the report, the size of the company, the internal personnel available to conduct an investigation and the extent to which they have training on how to do so, the person against whom the complaint is made, and resources available to conduct an investigation.

Let's walk through some key issues that are important in any scenario related to a report of harassment or discrimination. First, the leaders charged with responding to the complaint need to know and understand the employer's anti-harassment and anti-discrimination policy. Typically, a supervisor plays a role in that policy, which is that they can receive complaints and must take action to ensure the issue is handled.

What does that mean, and how should the issue be handled? Under the law, if an employee brings a complaint of harassment or discrimination, an employer has a duty to investigate it. How an employer does this is not a one-size-fits-all proposition, and it can look different based on the complaint, the size of the company, and what type of resources the employer has internally.

For example, with many organizations that have an HR Director, if a complaint is made to a supervisor, the appropriate response for the supervisor is to immediately loop HR in so the issue can be investigated. The key thing for the supervisor to know is that the complaint must be handled promptly and appropriately. The supervisor may need to facilitate communications with the employee and cooperate in an investigation. However, as long as a supervisor can recognize the importance of the issue and can pass the issue off to those who can get the investigation going, then the supervisor may well have fulfilled their obligations.

Sometimes, supervisors are confused about what an investigation is and why it is needed. Quite simply, the law requires an employer to investigate to make sure a complaint of harassment and/or discrimination is handled appropriately. This means the appropriate witnesses must be interviewed and must be given a fair opportunity to tell their version of the facts. It also means that the person doing the interviews must assess the credibility of these people. And, ultimately, it means that someone needs to gather enough facts and information so that the employer can determine whether the incident reported actually occurred and, if it did, exactly what happened. Hopefully, this information will be compiled in a written report. Once that occurs, the employer is required to take action, if needed, to ensure no further harassment or discrimination occurs. In recent times, the EEOC has prosecuted cases against employers who failed to adequately investigate a complaint, underscoring how failure to investigate can trigger legal liability.

More importantly, an investigation is the only way an employer can truly show that it made an effort to understand what happened and to ensure that if there was a problem, it was handled so that the employer was able to protect its employees and comply with the law.

There are a lot of nuances to investigations that we won't cover here, but one thing to keep in mind is that an investigation always needs to be handled by someone familiar with handling workplace investigations, as there are certain issues that an adequate investigation needs to address. Thus, a police officer who handles criminal investigations is not necessarily qualified to do this. A leader with no experience in workplace investigations should not just start making calls to talk to people without an understanding of the appropriate way an investigation should take place.

### Here are some of the key takeaways regarding workplace investigations:

- Every employer should have an adequate and up-to-date anti-harassment and anti-discrimination policy. Supervisors should be trained in this policy.

- Reports should be handled quickly, appropriately, and in accordance with the policy.

- Investigations should be handled by personnel trained in conducting workplace investigations and compiling reports. This could be internal human resource personnel, an outside workplace investigator, an HR consultant, or an employment lawyer.

- Employers should consider remedial measures when a report comes in. Should the alleged harasser be put on administrative leave pending investigation?

- Employers should be mindful of the workplace communications that go along with the report. This includes communications with the complainant and the employees who will be interviewed.

- Employers should obtain a written investigation report at the end of the investigation, which includes findings, conclusions, and credibility assessments.

- At the conclusion of the investigation, the investigation should be "closed out" by a notification to the complainant and to the alleged harasser.

# CHAPTER 8

# ADA Scope and Three Basic ADA Concepts Every Leader Needs to Know

Unlike the law of sexual discrimination and sexual harassment that most people are generally familiar with, the law of disability discrimination is not as widely known and understood. This law is very broad, and just like other areas of discrimination and harassment, it is constantly evolving and changing as time passes and social norms change.

## ADA Scope

Let's talk about the scope of the ADA. Stated simply, it is broad and it is the number one source of discrimination claims against employers. If an employee comes to you and expresses a concern that their medical condition is impacting their ability to get their job done, there is a high probability that their condition may qualify as a disability. Why? Because when Congress overhauled the ADA back in 2008, they intended it to be broad and they intended employers to give employees the benefit of the doubt when considering whether they suffered from a disability.

Here is an example of how this has played out. I have a daughter with Type 1 Diabetes, so this medical condition is of personal interest to me—I have spent fourteen years watching how difficult this medical condition is to live with and how it can be controlled one minute and life-threatening the next. When a person has Type 1, their pancreas no longer produces insulin, a hormone needed to convert food into energy. Theoretically, a person with Type 1 should be able to control it with insulin, but there are many factors that can make that control difficult to achieve. If a person with Type 1 gets too much insulin, they can die. Or, if they don't get enough insulin, they can die. As it turns out, trying to replicate what would normally be automatically controlled by an organ is difficult.

Before Congress overhauled the ADA in 2008, it was easier for an employer to deny an accommodation for an employee who sought coverage under the ADA for Type 1 when it impacted their ability to do their job. Based on the way the law used to be written, it was easier for an employer to challenge whether an employee was actually disabled or not, and an employee seeking an accommodation or other protections might have to take a case all the way to trial in order to obtain a ruling that they suffered from a disability and were entitled to accommodations. Congress realized that this was not the way the ADA was supposed to work, so the decision was made to overhaul it.

Through the amendments to the ADA in 2008, it became clear that disabilities like Type 1 are now covered. In fact, the message that was conveyed with the overhaul was that employers should not pick the fight over whether an employee suffers from a disability but rather should, instead, consider how the employer could work with the employee to see if there were ways to keep them on the job. The coverage under the ADA is broad, and there are strong arguments that most medical conditions are covered.

Sometimes, this broad coverage can be surprising. The ADA, like Title VII, applies to employers with fifteen or more employees. However, state law may trigger protections for employees with disabilities, even for smaller employers. For example, in the state where I live, there is a Human Rights Act with protections that mirror the ADA. However, our Human Rights Act is triggered for any employer with five or more employees. If you are an employer with fewer than fifteen employees, you need to know whether you have ADA (or similar obligations) based on state law protections.

## Specific Medical Conditions Covered Under the ADA

Let's talk about some specific medical conditions that are covered under the ADA—conditions that you might not think of as being a disability. Mental health, prescription drug addiction, and, in some cases, alcoholism can be covered, as well. Pregnancy, although also covered by the Pregnant Workers Fairness Act, can also have ADA implications.

For supervisors, this means that you need to be aware of the broad reach of the ADA. If an employee comes to you and reports an inability to do a job caused by a medical condition, you need to take that to HR or the person designated to handle issues like this, as there could be an ADA issue lurking in the background.

Some disabilities will be more obvious, and when that happens, it may trigger further obligations for an employer. For example, imagine an employee in the middle of chemotherapy, working through a cancer diagnosis. Obviously, if that employee comes to a supervisor and indicates they need help to get their regular job done, it will trigger obligations on the part of an employer. However, these same obligations may arise from mental and physical conditions that are not quite as easy to spot as falling under the ADA.

We will dig deeper into some of the more complex ADA issues. But for now, there are several concepts, terms, and phrases that every leader needs to know and understand when it comes to handling an ADA issue.

## Three Basic ADA Concepts

The three phrases that every leader needs to know and to be generally familiar with are "reasonable accommodation," "essential function," and "interactive process." Armed with basic knowledge about what these concepts mean, most employers can avoid an ADA claim.

### 1. Essential Functions

Generally speaking, the ADA provides protections to a qualified individual with a medical condition that impacts their ability to perform their job, so long as they can perform the essential functions of their position with or without reasonable accommodations.

Hang on—what do those terms and concepts mean? Obviously, in order to understand whether an employee is qualified for protection under the ADA, you need to understand what an essential function is and what a reasonable accommodation looks like. Don't worry; these concepts will come together quite easily, and once you have them down, you will be armed with the basic information you need to comply with the ADA.

The "essential functions" of a job are the primary duties each employee performs. One way to know what those duties and functions are is to look at a job description. This is one reason (although there are many) why you should have a job description and why you should keep it updated. Another way to figure out what an employee's primary duties are is by talking with the employee and their supervisor. Sometimes, in ADA cases, if there is no job description, this is an alternative way to find the answer to this question. How much time does an employee spend working on this task or duty? What would happen if the employee did not perform the task or duty? These are important questions that weigh into the analysis. If a function is rarely performed by the employee, even if it is in the job description, it may not be an essential function.

There is a case from several years ago that drives this concept home. This case involved a mechanic who applied for a job working in his field repairing trucks. The mechanic did not have a commercial driver's license (and could not get one) because he had Type 1 Diabetes. His application was declined because he could not get a license to drive the trucks. The mechanic was confused by the denial of his application because he did not want to drive trucks. Instead, he only wanted to repair them.

He filed a lawsuit claiming disability discrimination. As it turned out, the court agreed with the mechanic. When the parties did a deep dive into the essential functions of the job at issue, they discovered that employees performing the position that the mechanic applied for rarely had to drive the trucks they repaired. An issue might come up once or twice a year that required a mechanic to drive a truck, but even when that type of situation arose, there were other mechanics who worked at the shop who could do that. The court concluded that driving a truck (and needing a CDL) was not an essential function of that position. Thus, it was illegal for the company at issue to refuse to hire the employee on the alleged basis that he could not perform an essential function because of his disability.

This seems like a basic concept, but it is very important to have an understanding of what an essential function is in order for anyone to maneuver through the ADA.

You may wonder, "What happens if you do not have a job description?" There are other ways to figure out an employee's essential functions. That might include talking to other employees who perform the job, interviewing a supervisor, or even looking at a job posting to see what the key duties were at the time the position was filled. Some other helpful inquiries that help define the essential functions include the question,

"What would happen if the function was not performed?" If the answer is that it would not be a problem, then it is probably not an essential function. Another important question is, "Are there other employees available who could perform the function if the employee at issue was unable to?" If the answer is that there are, then it might not be an essential function at issue. The big takeaway here is that the essential functions are the primary duties an employee performs, and every employer should have a way to figure out what those primary duties are. On top of that, employers should figure out what those primary duties are before a problem arises, not after. So dust off those job descriptions to make sure they are updated, and if they are not, get them into shape now.

## 2. Reasonable Accommodation

Reasonable accommodations are assistance or modifications given by the employer to the employee in order to make it so the employee can do their job. Help can take many forms, all depending on the job at issue, the size of the employer, and the medical condition that is impairing the employee's ability to do their job. The concept of help is not a difficult one, but what makes the ADA tricky to maneuver through is that the type of help an employer is required to give differs based on a number of different factors. There is no manual describing all potential reasonable accommodations available because, at the end of the day, there are so many of them that it would be impossible to come up with all the different accommodations. For example, imagine an employee suffering from depression who works as a creative designer for an employer with 100 employees. That employee may need accommodations that are very different from those that an employer might be required to give to a firefighter with a back injury. Every situation is going to be different based on the employee's medical condition, the size of the employer, and the employee's job.

Some types of accommodations, like providing a better chair for an employee with a back disability or providing a slight schedule change in order for an employee seeing a mental health counselor to attend doctor's appointments, may seem fairly easy to analyze. In fact, if the accommodation is easy to grant, and if the request seems straightforward, it might make sense in many cases for the employer to just grant it without going through a lengthy process (and then to document that the employer did so).

However, with more complex accommodation requests that stand to disrupt the workplace, impact the way the employee's job is done, or cost the employer substantial time and money, it makes sense for an employer to go through a structured process. For example, imagine an employee who works the front desk and who approaches their employer with a request to work remotely due to a diagnosis of depression or anxiety. Chances are the accommodation request, if granted, would change the way the front desk position functions and would likely require other personnel to take time out of their role to cover for the front desk person. Is this a reasonable request? The answer to that question depends on a number of factors, including whether the employee performs other duties that can be performed at home, whether the employee's healthcare provider can establish that the requested accommodation would enable the employee to perform the essential functions of their job, and whether the employer has other personnel who could cover any gaps in the employee's position caused by the remote work request.

These are not easy questions to answer, which is why there is a recommended process each employer should go through when a request like this comes in. We will walk through this process in the next section entitled "The ADA Interactive Process."

## 3. The ADA Interactive Process

Under the ADA, the focus is on the employer working in a good faith interactive process with the employee to see if there is a way to keep the employee on the job and working despite limitations caused by a medical condition. This basically means that employers should focus on discussions and communications with disabled employees to see if there are reasonable accommodations available. This process will be driven by the employer and usually includes information sharing: The employer will let the employee know what information they are seeking, and the employee will need to provide the information.

The best way to understand what this process looks like is to walk through it from start to finish. Several weeks ago, one of our clients, a supervisor named Miriam, contacted us with an ADA issue. Sarah, an on-site bookkeeper, was asking for the ability to work from home. She had recently been diagnosed with fibromyalgia and complained that she was in pain, had trouble walking, and needed extra time to perform tasks that she had previously been able to do. Miriam was unsure what to do, so we walked her through the process from start to finish. It looked like this…

First, we told Miriam to open an ADA file. With ADA issues, confidentiality is important, and an employer needs to keep ADA information separate from the personnel file. It is also important to limit communications to those leaders who need to be privy to the situation. Frequently, this might include the HR Director, the supervisor, and the employee. What an employer never wants to do is openly discuss the employee's issue with leaders who are not part of a process or, even worse, with co-workers who should not be involved in the process.

Miriam was then directed to provide Sarah with an ADA accommodation letter—a letter that basically says the employer is working to comply with the ADA and is writing to engage in the ADA interactive process. This is one of the most important parts of the process, so do not skip this step! The letter will list the essential functions of the employee's job and will ask the healthcare provider to suggest reasonable accommodations. The letter will tell Sarah when she needs to return this information (usually, employers will ask for it to be returned in 2-3 weeks), and it will tell her who she should return the letter to. A copy of the letter was to be placed in Sarah's ADA file.

The ADA does not provide many tools to the employer as part of the process, but the ability to ask the employee for information from a healthcare provider is expressly allowed. In fact, if you think about it, how else would an employer know which essential functions are impacted by an employee's medical condition, and how else would an employer know what accommodations would help the employee to overcome the limitations? Sometimes, employers try to apply their own life experience or guess as to the answers to these questions, but that is a big mistake. Get the information from the person who is knowledgeable about this—the healthcare provider!

Let's talk about Sarah's request to work from home as a result of her fibromyalgia. In order for Miriam to consider what reasonable accommodations are out there, she needs to consider how Sarah's fibromyalgia impacts her ability to perform the essential functions of her job. However, Miriam does not have the medical expertise needed to make that call, and the ADA does not require her to guess at or research this. While it is true that Sarah might have some opinions as to how her fibromyalgia is impacting her, the ADA entitles Miriam to get a healthcare professional's opinion on this. So Miriam definitely needs to do this. It is the best way to better understand Sarah's limitations and to figure out what factors will drive the consideration of reasonable accommodations and would enable her to stay on the job performing the essential functions of her position.

Miriam did as we advised and gave Sarah the ADA accommodation letter. However, Miriam called us a month later and said the process was not going well. Although she had given Sarah three weeks to obtain the answers from her doctor, Sarah told Miriam about three weeks in that she was going to need more time. Miriam gave her an additional two weeks to get the information from her healthcare provider. This is not unusual, and the ADA requires an employer to give an employee a reasonable amount of time to obtain the healthcare information. So, by giving her another two weeks, Miriam had done the right thing. In fact, depending on the circumstances, there may be times when an employer has to allow multiple extensions on the return of the healthcare provider's information. This can be frustrating to employers who are trying to move the process forward. However, the reality is that the process may take months to complete, and the ADA requires the employer to provide the employee with a reasonable amount of time to move through the various steps of the process. An employer frequently will not be able to control how quickly the process can be completed.

Miriam had other concerns, too. When Sarah returned the information, she brought in a letter from a physician's assistant, not a physician, and it did not go through which essential functions were impacted by her fibromyalgia. Instead, the letter Sarah brought in merely said, "Sarah has been diagnosed with fibromyalgia, and she needs to work remotely from time to time." Miriam wondered what she was supposed to do in light of the inadequate information returned to her.

We told Miriam to be patient and reassured her that this frequently is the path this phase of the accommodation process follows. Unfortunately, it was going to take a little more legwork on Miriam's part. We directed Miriam to document what had transpired to date in a letter that she was going to give to Sarah (and that she would ultimately place in the ADA file). The letter should recite the dates she and Sarah had spoken, the date Sarah was given the initial letter, and the date she came back with the letter from her physician's assistant. It should then say that Sarah had not returned adequate information and that Miriam was asking Sarah to return to her doctor to obtain answers to the questions outlined in the letter. Alternatively, if Sarah was willing to execute a medical release, she could work with Miriam to arrange a call with Sarah's healthcare provider so Miriam could go over the questions directly with the healthcare provider. At any rate, the message to Sarah needed to be that while there were several ways she could meet her ADA obligation to provide information from a healthcare provider, she had not yet satisfied her obligations, and her employer was not able to identify reasonable accommodations until she had done so.

Sarah went back to her healthcare provider and ultimately returned information detailing which functions were impacted. However, the healthcare provider did not provide much input about accommodations, indicating, instead, that working from home was the only reasonable accommodation that would enable Sarah to do her job.

We discussed this with Miriam and told her that the ADA does not always require an employer to provide the accommodation requested by the employee. Instead, if there are other reasonable accommodations that will enable the employee to perform the essential functions, then those accommodations should be considered, too. Miriam wondered if there were other accommodations out there, other than working from home, that would apply to an employee with fibromyalgia. We told her about a great online resource called JAN—the Job Accommodation Network. This resource provides various accommodations that an employer can search by medical condition. When Miriam did this, she found a number of alternative accommodations and learned more about the different ways fibromyalgia can impact an employee in the workplace. The information Miriam found enabled her to have a discussion with Sarah about other potential accommodations that could apply. We advised Miriam to document these conversations and to make sure the process she followed and the conversations she had with Sarah were recorded in a document that landed in the ADA file.

This is one example of how the ADA process can look from start to finish. There are many variations of this that play out in real life.

*The key takeaways when working through the ADA process are as follows:*

- Set up an ADA file and keep related documentation and information in this file. Record dates of communications and meetings and keep emails related to the accommodation process in this file.

- Maintain confidentiality throughout the process by only involving the leaders who need to be involved in the process.

- Communicate with the employee and take prompt action to get the interactive process started. Keep the employee informed throughout the process as to the status of the accommodation.

- Obtain information from the employee's healthcare provider in order to get an understanding as to how the medical condition at issue impacts the employee's ability to perform the essential functions of their job and in order to get input on potential reasonable accommodations.

- When it comes to reasonable accommodations, keep in mind that the employer has to grant a reasonable accommodation. However, the employer is not necessarily obligated to provide the reasonable accommodation sought by the employee if other reasonable accommodations exist. Consult JAN to get ideas on the full range of reasonable accommodations.

# CHAPTER 9

# Alcoholism and Drug Addiction

Two of the most difficult issues for employers to handle in accordance with the law are alcoholism and drug addiction by employees. This could involve a situation where an employee appears impaired in the workplace. It could involve a situation where an employee gets arrested. It could involve a situation where an employee's performance starts to take a nosedive. There are so many ways an issue like this might surface that I cannot even begin to identify them all. But what I can say with nearly 100% confidence is that if an employer does not do a deep dive into the law of the ADA on situations involving drug or alcohol use, they will likely end up dealing with a claim or a lawsuit. I have helped multiple employers defend lawsuits involving these types of issues, and I have seen firsthand how emotional these types of issues can be, how the law is unclear and confusing, and how there are so many potential pitfalls awaiting any employer who tries to maneuver through these issues. It is dangerous territory, for sure.

Let me give you an example of what I am talking about. Dan worked as a heavy equipment operator, and for the first two years of his employment, his supervisors thought he was good at what he did and that he was a good employee. However, Dan started to undergo some personality changes. First, he started to develop a negative attitude. He began to criticize his supervisor and make comments about what a bad job his supervisor was doing. Where he used to spend his breaks talking with his co-workers, he began to withdraw, avoiding others and spending his breaks in his car. Although Dan used to have a good attendance record, on several occasions, he no-showed. On one occasion, his supervisor called him at home and asked if he was coming in. Dan indicated that he had overslept and came to work an hour and a half late. This was a major departure from his typical work ethic.

Dan's supervisor, Pete, met with him to inquire what was going on. Dan confessed that he had been having trouble getting his prescriptions filled. He indicated that he was taking oxycodone to help him cope with Post-Traumatic Stress Disorder (PTSD) he suffered from serving as a veteran in Iraq. In addition, he suffered a back injury when he was in the military and suffered some ongoing pain.

Pete was alarmed. This came as news to him—he had no idea Dan was taking oxycodone. Pete was worried that, as a heavy equipment operator, Dan posed a safety risk to himself, to his co-workers, and to the public to the extent he was driving his equipment in and about the public area in which he worked. Pete's employer had a number of safety policies, and oxycodone use violated them. Pete contacted HR, and together, they approached Dan and told him he would need to provide documentation from his physician, establishing that Dan had a valid prescription for oxycodone and could safely perform his job. All told, they gave Dan nearly eight weeks to get the information from his doctor, but Dan was unable to do so. At the end of that time period, Pete fired Dan. Dan filed a disability discrimination against his former employer.

Six years later, after depositions, numerous court briefings, two separate lawsuits, and numerous rounds of briefing and argument, Dan's case was finally resolved. Why did it take so long? Because the law in this area is sparse and very fact-specific, all depending on the employee at issue, the employer at issue, the job position at issue, and even the safety protocols in place by the employer. Further complicating matters is timing: when and how the employer was alerted to the problem, how the employer dealt with the problem, how long they gave the employee to get the information from his doctor, and when and how the employer fired the employee. All of this matters.

Dan's situation is a difficult one, raising many important questions. Was Dan addicted to oxycodone? Was he unsafe to himself or others? Was Dan taking oxycodone without a valid prescription? Was he impaired while he was working for the employer? Dan's employer did not have definitive answers to these questions at the time they fired him, and therein lies the problem.

While it is possible that the answer to all of these questions was yes, it is very important that any time an employer has noticed that an employee is working while they are impaired by a drug or that they pose a safety issue, the employer needs to seek legal assistance or otherwise find someone able to dig deep to help come up with a plan that complies with the law. Let's talk about some of the key considerations any time drugs or alcohol are at issue.

## 1. Performance

Performance matters in every ADA discrimination claim. Before an employer takes any adverse action against an employee based on a suspected ADA problem, the employer needs to figure out what type of documents show a valid performance concern. Dan claimed that he was performing just fine at the time of his termination and that there was no evidence that he was impaired on the job. Luckily, Pete had documented the meeting he had with Dan to discuss the attitude, the attendance problems, the change in behavior, and the performance issues. However, this highlights how important it is for an employer to document the situation any time an employee starts to undergo a significant performance change or commits a major policy breach. The documentation can be in the form of a coaching email or even a memo to the file—it does not need to be in a formal disciplinary document. Here, Pete's conversations with HR about Dan were also documented, and all of this became important evidence in the case. One of the biggest mistakes an employer can make is to ignore a significant performance problem—especially if it involves something as important as on-the-job drug or alcohol use by an employee working in a safety-sensitive job.

Why does it matter, and what happens if the employer does not document performance? One thing that can happen is that it can raise the question of whether or not the employer had a legitimate reason to be worried about safety, to think that there was a performance issue, and, ultimately, to move forward with termination. We call this pretext in the employment law world. Did the employer really think there was a safety or performance problem, or is the employer making it up to fire the employee for some other reason related to their disability? Solid documentation goes a long way to show the performance issue was real.

You will notice there is a repeat theme in this book. Anytime an employer does not document a performance issue and then subsequently terminates the employee, it opens the door for an employee to argue that an employer is acting for a discriminatory reason. That is, it opens the door for an employee to argue that an employer does not like disabled employees or is otherwise acting unlawfully. Here, Dan argued that his employer was out to fire veterans and that his supervisor was trying to exact revenge upon him because Dan had gone to HR several months before to complain about the supervisor. If Pete had not documented the change in performance, Dan could have gotten some traction on those issues. I can't emphasize enough—document performance problems!

Sometimes, supervisors will complain that it is unrealistic for them to draft a write-up every time an employee they supervise does something wrong. Fair enough. However, documentation does not always need to be in a formal, written warning. Even emails documenting coaching issues can suffice to show a problem existed.

## 2. The Job Description and the Policies At Issue

Another important question an employer needs to understand when it is considering discipline based on suspected drug or alcohol use is what are the duties the employee must perform in their position, and what policies have been triggered based on the suspected drug or alcohol use? Here, Dan was a heavy equipment operator, and that raised safety concerns since his job description made it very clear that his job was a safety-sensitive position due to his daily contact with the public. It made it clear that he was not allowed to take any drugs that impaired his ability to perform, and it clarified that he was required to maintain a Commercial Driver's License.

However, not every employee performs a safety-sensitive function. With Dan, it was easy for the employer to recognize an immediate threat to public safety, as well as a threat to Dan and his co-workers, if he was performing his job while impaired. But what if an employee has a job where they are not required to drive and where they do not interact with the public? This factors into what actions an employer can or cannot take, and it is important for an employer to think through the essential functions of the employee's job before they make a decision based on drug or alcohol use.

Based on Dan's position, various safety policies were also invoked, and it was important for Dan's employer to have all of these laid out for consideration, too. Some employers have separate safety policies that might be triggered by an employee who is impaired on the job. If so, the employer needs to pull these out, analyze them, and consider how the situation at hand plays into them. If an employer is going to make an argument that an employee drinking or doing drugs on the job creates a huge safety risk, then the employer better be able to explain what policies are triggered by this and how the employer considered them in regard to whatever action they ultimately took.

## 3. Drug and Alcohol Testing Policies

An employer's drug and alcohol testing policies are also potentially placed at issue any time there is a concern that an employee is impaired by drugs or alcohol while on the job. While most employers have a drug and alcohol policy, the reality is that many employers have never actually had to use their policy. On the one hand, this is good—many employers have never had a situation where they had to actually get an employee transported to a testing facility in order to analyze whether or not they were impaired by drugs or alcohol on the job.

On the other hand, this is a problem, as it could result in a situation where supervisors (or even HR) do not know what protocol to follow if a situation arises where the supervisor needs to get an employee tested. That is why every employer should give their drug and alcohol testing policy some thought before a problem arises. For example, every employer should know when testing is appropriate, who will perform the test, what drugs will be tested for, how the sample will be obtained, what process to follow to get the testing done, and what to do while the results are pending.

Although this seems like it would be straightforward, I know firsthand from a case I worked on that it is not. In that case, the employee (like Dan) was suspected of being under the influence of oxycodone while in the workplace. The employer knew that the employee had recently had surgery and believed that the employee had a valid prescription. The employer had a drug and alcohol testing policy in place and had a third party lined up to do the testing.

However, when the employee showed up at work under the influence, the employer did not have him tested for a number of reasons. One was that the employer had a protocol where every employee was asked, at the time they were tested, if they were taking any prescription medications. If the employee indicated they were, and if the employee was able to prove that there was a valid prescription in place, then, according to the testing protocol, even if the employee tested positive for an impairing substance, the employee's test would indicate there was not a violation so long as the substance was one where the employee had a valid prescription. In that situation, the employer believed it made little sense for them to go through the hassle of testing the employee since the employee would probably be able to produce a valid prescription. This is a conversation every employer should have with the third party who conducts their testing: Every employer needs to know what substances are being tested for and what happens if an employee indicates they have a valid prescription for a substance that is part of the testing panel.

Timing is also an issue when it comes to drug and alcohol testing. What if a co-worker witnesses conduct in the workplace indicating that a worker is impaired but does not come forward to report the concern until many hours later? Will the passage of time impact the outcome of the drug and alcohol test? Or, what if a co-worker comes forward voicing a concern about a worker's impairment, but HR, who would normally arrange for the drug test, is out sick for the day? Is there a backup, and if so, what protocol needs to be followed to get the test performed? These issues demonstrate how important it is for an employer to have worked through every detail relating to the employer's drug and alcohol testing program.

Last of all, a word of caution on the issue of drug and alcohol testing. In some jurisdictions, the law is in flux on what type of workplace drug testing is allowed and what the significance of a positive drug test means. As you are reviewing your drug and alcohol testing policy, make sure you are considering new changes in both federal and state-specific laws, and consult with counsel if needed.

### 4. The ADA Interactive Process

The issue of whether drugs and alcohol are covered by the ADA is a challenging one. As a general rule, illegal drug use is not covered by the ADA. However, some prescription drug use may well be covered, and recovering drug users or alcoholics may be covered by the ADA, too. Any time an employee comes to an employer disclosing a drug or alcohol problem, the employer should seek legal counsel due to the complexities of the law in this area. I have worked on a handful of ADA disability discrimination cases stemming from drug use or alcohol use that impacted an employee's ability to do their job, and what I can say with certainty is that these cases are very fact-dependent and are full of pitfalls for employers who are trying to maneuver through the various laws in play. That being said, if the employer recognizes that the ADA might be at issue (and analyzes options under the ADA) before they make decisions impacting the employee, they will likely be okay. It is the employers who fail to consider the ADA at all who end up with the most liability.

While the regular ADA process we have discussed above will likely come into play when drugs or alcohol are involved, there may be some different considerations, too. For example, timing may be more critical if suspected drug or alcohol use is at issue. The following questions should be considered if an employee is suspected of on-the-job drug or alcohol use or impairment:

1. **Is there a chance the employee has a valid prescription that would cause impairment?** If so, the employer is obligated to consider reasonable accommodations, so a conversation with the employee aimed at better understanding the situation may well be the first step to occur.

2. **Should the employer perform immediate drug or alcohol testing based on the employer's policy?** Obviously, time is always of the essence when it comes to whether or not drug or alcohol use will show up in a test. Do the circumstances justify such a test? What

do the employer's policies say? Have concerns of impairment been substantiated? Has the employee indicated that they have a valid prescription that may result in a positive hit? If an employee has indicated that they have a valid prescription, then this will be an important consideration if drug or alcohol testing is performed.

3. *Is the employee's safety at risk if they are impaired on the job? Is the health or safety of co-workers at risk? What about the health or safety of the public?* If the answer to any of these questions is yes, the employer should get counsel on the line and consider whether the employee should be put on paid leave to get them out of the workplace and to ensure safety. Any time an employee is removed from the workplace, there is a different type of risk involved, so decisions like this one should not be made lightly. However, if an employee is impaired and is performing a safety-sensitive job, immediate measures to ensure the employee, their co-workers, and the public are protected should be considered.

4. *What type of discussion should occur in regard to accommodations?* If an employee is lawfully using a prescription that impairs their performance, accommodations may be required. However, an employer will not generally be required to excuse essential functions, lower job performance standards, or excuse illegal drug use.

Depending on the job performed by the employee, some more complex issues under the ADA may arise in the context of drug or alcohol use. These include a direct threat assessment or a fitness-for-duty examination. These concepts go somewhat beyond the scope of this book but know that in some limited circumstances, an employer has the ability to remove an employee from the workplace and/or to obtain additional information about an employee's ability to do their job. These concepts should be explored with counsel based on the specific facts at issue.

## 5. Supervisor Training—If You See Something, Say Something

Anytime you have a long-time employee, the risk goes up if you move forward with discipline or a termination. Why? Because the presumption is that if you liked the employee enough to let them stay for multiple decades, they must be doing a good job performing. Of course, that may not be the case. Maybe the supervisor just did not do a good job of flagging performance deficiencies and coaching the employee to improve. Maybe the supervisor did not have time to manage the employee. Maybe the supervisor felt overwhelmed and did not know what to say or how to raise the issue of a performance problem. We have already touched on why it is so important for your supervisors to be trained. However, the issue of a supervisor raising a performance problem, if one exists, is very important in the context of how an employer should manage a drug and alcohol problem. If the supervisor does not document performance deficiencies, it makes it very difficult for an employer to terminate an employee without drawing a claim.

Take this example. Bill has managed Shawn for ten years and has never told him that he is not performing well. However, Bill frequently talks to other managers about how bad of a performer Shawn is and talks about wanting to terminate him to make his crew more effective.

One day, Bill approaches Shawn to talk about a project, and Shawn slurs his words during the course of their conversation. Bill does not do anything about it. He thinks that Shawn has had a tough home life and gives him the benefit of the doubt that this is a "one-off." The following week, Bill is talking to Shawn and notices that he smells like alcohol. Again, Bill is not sure what to do and does not want to overreact. Bill asks James, Shawn's friend and co-worker, if he smells anything, and James says he does not. Bill decides it is not worth the trouble to take it any further.

Supervisors are held to a higher standard, and Bill's conduct will have numerous ramifications in the subsequent lawsuit Shawn brings against the employer when he is fired several weeks later for workplace impairment. First, Bill has shown he is not complying with the employer's safety policies, code of conduct provisions, and drug and alcohol testing policy. By his inaction, Bill has just opened the door for the attorney representing Shawn to argue that the policies in place at the employer's business were not followed and opens the door for the attorney to argue that the supervisors do not know the basics of the law.

In addition, Bill's lackadaisical reaction to Shawn's impairment in the workplace makes it look like safety and performance issues were not a concern for the employer. After all, if Bill knew about the issue and did nothing, it must not have been that important. On top of that, by Bill ignoring the drug and alcohol testing policy, the employer does not have any concrete evidence to show that Shawn was under the influence at work, while the drug and alcohol test may have provided such evidence. Even more importantly, it will now be very difficult for the employer to argue that Shawn was not performing his job adequately since the only evidence the employer has of this is Bill's word.

Supervisor inaction makes it difficult for an employer to justify a termination decision, and we have had multiple cases where a supervisor's failure to spot an issue and/or to take action based on it ultimately cost the employer the ability to defend the case.

## 6. Placing an Employee on Leave Pending a Decision

If an employee appears to be under the influence of drugs and/or alcohol in the workplace, it makes sense for the employer to think through whether they remove the employee from the workplace, pending further investigation and analysis. This is especially true if the employee poses a threat. For example, in the situation described above with Dan, the heavy equipment operator taking oxycodone, if safety truly is an issue, then it might make sense to place Dan on paid leave pending further analysis. One thing you can count on with the ADA is that the analysis may take some time to complete—especially if additional input from medical providers is required. Leaving Dan on the job pending a decision sends a message that safety is not that important. In addition, it could cause risk for the company if they are on notice of a potential issue but do nothing to alleviate the risk.

Placing an employee on leave requires some consideration and some documentation. Any time an employer places an employee on unpaid leave pending an investigation it is risky, as that could qualify as an adverse action and give rise to a legal claim. The safest route is always going to be to place an employee on paid leave, not unpaid leave. I understand the frustration this causes employers, and I frequently get pushback from my clients because they are frustrated at the amount of money a period of paid leave will cost the company. However, if the case turns into a claim or a lawsuit, you can rest assured that any amount the company saves by placing an employee on unpaid leave pending a decision will easily be surpassed by the cost the company will incur to resolve the lawsuit. I have worked with numerous employers who have regretted the decision to go with a period of unpaid leave—it is simply too risky. Why create an adverse action before you ultimately know all of the facts? The answer is you should not—going with paid leave is the best route.

Documentation is important whenever you place someone on paid leave. This does not need to be a long or complicated document. Instead, the goal is simply to convey that the employee is on a period of paid leave, the applicable dates of when their leave begins and when you anticipate it will end, that they should not work (or contact co-workers) during that period, that their assistance and cooperation may be needed to gather information, and that they will be notified as soon as a decision has been reached.

## 7. Interplay With FMLA

Do not forget about the Family Medical Leave Act (FMLA)! It is possible that if an employer is dealing with a situation involving drug or alcohol use or addiction, the employee may seek (or has already sought) FMLA leave. Whenever the ADA intersects with the FMLA, the analysis becomes even more complex, so employers need to be on the lookout for situations where overlap could arise.

For example, what if, on Monday, an employee approaches HR about taking a period of FMLA leave to get treatment for a prescription opioid addiction? While HR is getting the paperwork in place, the employee's supervisor becomes concerned that the employee appears impaired. On Tuesday, the supervisor (who does not know the employee is about to take FMLA leave) terminates the employee for suspected impairment. Hopefully, you recognize that there are many problems with that scenario (since, in this scenario, the supervisor does not appear to be considering accommodation). However, since the supervisor did not loop in the HR personnel with knowledge about the request for FMLA leave, the employer is now looking not only at an ADA claim but an FMLA interference claim, as well.

Good communication can help an employer to avoid situations like this one. We previously covered the importance of running through a checklist any time a supervisor is considering termination. If that had happened here, the supervisor hopefully would have involved others with relevant information and, by doing so, would have come across information showing the employee was taking FMLA leave. On top of that, hopefully, by looking at the checklist, the supervisor would have become aware that the employee may have a potential disability and would have pumped the brakes on that account, too.

When an employee takes FMLA leave for a serious medical condition, it can serve as notice to the employer that the employee may have some type of disability. If the employee has taken FMLA because of their medical condition, then, at the completion of the period of FMLA leave, the employer may need to perform a separate analysis as to whether the employee is entitled to a reasonable accommodation when they return from FMLA leave. Some employers make the mistake of thinking that if an employer provides FMLA leave for an employee, then the employer's obligations end there. Not so. In many employment law scenarios, an employer is obligated to provide FMLA leave, and the ADA analysis will not occur until the employee has returned from the period of FMLA leave (except in intermittent FMLA leave scenarios). It is essential for employers to know that even after the FMLA obligations are satisfied, if the employer is on notice of the employee's serious medical condition, then the employer may well have an obligation to engage in an ADA analysis and to provide reasonable accommodations, too.

# CHAPTER 10

# Mental Health and Complex Issues Like Suicide

While some disabilities may be obvious, others are not. In recent years, the EEOC has clarified that depression, anxiety, PTSD, and bipolar disorder are all covered under the ADA. This presents some challenges for employers, as these can be invisible disabilities without any obvious symptoms. Aside from drug and alcohol use, mental health disabilities provide some of the most challenging ADA issues that employers must work through, and it is very important that supervisors know and understand some key concepts related to this.

A situation that we worked through with one of our clients, Mark, shows just how complex working through mental health disabilities can be. Mark supervised Jason, a long-time employee. For many years, Jason, who was well-known in the community as a leader of Mark's organization, was a solid performer. Jason served on numerous boards and spoke at many industry conferences. However, last year, all of that changed, and Jason's performance started to decline. His demeanor became unpredictable: sometimes he was friendly, sometimes he was borderline rude. Jason began to pull out of his community involvement, and it got back to Mark that Jason no-showed at some of his speaking events.

Mark was unsure of what was happening, but before he had a chance to sit down with Jason to discuss his concerns, Mark was notified that Jason was suicidal and that law enforcement had been called by Jason's family members because they feared he was going to make an attempt on his life. Mark was worried that if Jason was suicidal, he would not be able to perform his job. He was worried that if news of Mark's mental health condition got out, it could harm the company's reputation. He wondered if he needed to act quickly to terminate Jason to avoid any type of associational hit by the company.

Luckily, Mark contacted us, and we were able to help him work through the ADA interactive process before he made any decisions or took any action that could create liability under the ADA. We told Mark that he needed more information from a healthcare provider before he had enough information to assess the situation. We cautioned against acting upon stereotypes or assumptions and talked about how there was no evidence to show that Jason's encounter with law enforcement was publicly available or that it would harm the company. We talked about the importance of acting upon objective information instead of fears or assumptions. Mark's situation was an extreme one. However, it shows how some employers can be caught off guard by the broad scope of mental health coverage under the ADA. To add to the complexity of issues like this, the outcome here could have been different if Jason was a law enforcement officer carrying a gun or filled some other type of high-risk position where a mental health crisis may have rendered him unable to perform the essential functions of his position.

Depression and anxiety are also covered under the ADA, as are medical conditions like bipolar disorder and PTSD. These conditions require the same consideration of reasonable accommodations required by other medical conditions, meaning that employers should follow the same process we have identified above. Notably, employers should make sure to request information from the employer's healthcare provider to ascertain which essential functions are impacted, whether a requested accommodation would resolve limitations, and whether other reasonable accommodations are available. When it comes to mental health conditions, we sometimes see scenarios where the employer applies its own experience and guesses or surmises which essential functions are impacted and which accommodations would be reasonable. This is a bad idea, as there is no one-size-fits-all with mental health conditions. And, just because one person experienced some symptoms at a specific level of severity, it does not mean that someone else is going to experience the same thing. Employers should always leave it to the healthcare provider to describe limitations and to propose accommodations. And, for the purpose of spotting issues, every supervisor needs to recognize that mental health issues are covered under the ADA, and if an employee's ability to perform their job is impacted, then reasonable accommodations should be considered.

CHAPTER 11

# The Pregnant Workers Fairness Act

Jessica, who runs the front desk at a law firm, walked into her supervisor's office and asked for some time off. She explained that she and her partner had decided to undergo fertility treatments, and she would need time off in the coming months for doctor's appointments.

Danielle, on the other hand, who works in sales, had a baby several months ago and recently returned to work after taking parental leave. She approached her supervisor and told him that she needed a schedule change that would allow her to begin her workday later. She indicated that she is suffering from severe post-partum depression and would also like her performance quotas to be suspended while she is obtaining treatment for her depression.

Would the supervisors in your workplace be able to identify these as issues covered by the Pregnant Workers Fairness Act (PWFA)? Would they know and understand that the PWFA requires reasonable accommodations in a variety of situations, including situations like these?

Several years ago, an employer's legally-required response to these situations would have been different than what it is now. As to the employee seeking accommodations for fertility treatments, it is questionable whether those would have been protected under the ADA, and it is unlikely that accommodations would have been required. As to the employee suffering post-partum depression, she likely would have qualified for protections under the ADA related to a mental health disability. However, under the ADA, there would have been no obligation for the employer to suspend performance quotas if she was unable to perform the essential functions of her job. Not so, under the PWFA, as the suspension of performance quotes for a temporary period of time may well be reasonable.

The newly enacted PWFA, which went into effect in late 2023, is a broad statute focusing on reasonable accommodations. It contains some elements borrowed from the ADA, Title VII, and even the Providing Urgent Maternal Protections for Nursing Mothers Act (PUMP ACT), and is an expansive law aimed at enabling workers with a wide array of limitations to obtain reasonable accommodations in order to remain in the workplace. It requires a covered entity to provide reasonable accommodations to a qualified employee's or applicant's known limitations related to, affected by, or arising out of a pregnancy, childbirth, or related medical condition unless the accommodations will cause an undue hardship.

As you can tell from the language, the scope is wide. Don't be misled by the title. This statute does not just protect pregnant employees but also entitles employees suffering from many other types of medical conditions to accommodations before, during, and after pregnancy. Some of the conditions may already be covered by the ADA; some are not. Nevertheless, employees with many different types of temporary conditions will now be entitled to a reasonable accommodation when they did not previously qualify for such protections.

The PWFA, and the rules that clarify its requirements, state that reasonable accommodations may include additional, longer, or more flexible breaks; an allowance to use different types of equipment; alterations to work schedules; time off; light duty; or temporary reassignment. In fact, unlike the ADA, there are very specific examples given in the PWFA of accommodations that will likely be reasonable and for which employers should not request documentation before granting.

The PWFA even places restrictions on when an employer can request documentation in order to analyze a reasonable accommodation request and provides a narrow approach as to what type of documentation can be requested. Recall that under the ADA, an employer, in most circumstances, is allowed to request documentation as part of the interactive process in order for the employer to understand the employee's limitations on their ability to perform the essential functions and explore reasonable accommodations.

However, under the PWFA, the documentation itself must be reasonable and must not exceed the minimum amount of information needed to confirm the limitation, confirm that the limitation is related to pregnancy, childbirth, or a related condition, and describe a needed accommodation. Employers should not, under the PWFA, require ADA or FMLA-like forms, and the employee is not required to provide the employer with a medical diagnosis. The big take-away here is that employers need to approach accommodations under the PWFA on a case-by-case basis. There may be some situations where the requested accommodation is complex and would likely cause undue hardship for the employer. In such a case, documentation may be reasonable and may make sense. Nevertheless, that will not hold true in every case. For example, imagine if an employee seeks to have her workstation moved closer to a bathroom because she is suffering nausea. This is the type of accommodation that, under the PWFA, is so basic that an employer should not require any additional documentation from the employee.

In addition, under the PWFA, there are other accommodations that are so basic that if an employee indicates they are pregnant and requests one of these accommodations, the employer is expected to grant them without seeking or obtaining documentation. This includes modifications to the dress code or uniforms, minor modifications to the workplace or the workstation, allowing an employee to use a workstation closer to the bathroom, allowing an employee to use a closer parking place, allowing an employee to eat or drink at places where that is not typically allowed, and the allowance of personal protective equipment (PPE). Other areas where seeking documentation is prohibited include lactation, "basic, inexpensive, and commonly known" accommodation requests, and situations where employers without limitations would already receive such accommodations under the employer's policies.

Going back to the example of Danielle, the sales employee who sought to have her performance quotas suspended. Another major departure from the ADA is that under the PWFA, an employee may still be qualified to do their job even if they are not able to perform the essential functions of their position. This is true so long as the employee's inability to perform is temporary, the essential function can be performed in the near future, and the inability to perform can be reasonably accommodated by the employer without undue hardship. This is very different from the ADA, which does not require an employer to provide a reasonable accommodation to an employee who cannot perform the essential functions of their job.

Even production standards, which an employer would not typically be required to waive under the ADA, are treated differently under the PWFA. Instead, under the PWFA, an employer should not penalize an employee for lower productivity, focus, availability, or contribution if the lower production is due to a reasonable accommodation.

Under the PWFA, employers are expected to act quickly when an employee makes an accommodation request, and the PWFA makes it clear that it is not appropriate for an employer to make an employee wait while the accommodation request is considered. If time is needed for an employer to analyze a request, the PWFA encourages interim accommodations in order to avoid the risk of harm or danger to the employee so that an employee is not made to wait an extensive period of time for an answer. It may be that an employer needs to grant an accommodation on a temporary basis, document that this is the case, and then complete the analysis in order to make a final determination on whether it is an undue hardship that would result in the accommodation being withdrawn.

The big takeaway here is this: This law is new, and it's different than any law we have had on the books, too. If your in-house leaders are not trained in their obligations pursuant to this law, then they need training now to get their brains around the requirements of the PWFA.

### Here are some key takeaways to keep in mind.

- First, obvious conditions related to current, past, or intended pregnancy or related conditions must be accommodated. If it is easy to accommodate, you should do it.

- Be careful about asking for documentation from a medical provider. There are certain situations where the PWFA prohibits employers from seeking documentation.

- Employers are expected to act quickly, and the relatively new concept of interim accommodations is part of the PWFA.

Employers should be careful of the links between the PWFA and the ADA, Title VII, and the PUMP Act. In some cases, such as the previously cited example involving a new mother suffering from post-partum depression, there may be overlap between multiple statutes. In that case, undoubtedly, both the ADA and the PWFA would apply. When that is the case, employers should make sure they are offering the maximum protections/entitlements allowed to their employees. Employers should also double-check their handbooks to ensure the relevant policies and protocols are updated to address the PWFA.

The PWFA applies to applicants, as well as employees, so employers should consider how an applicant would know and understand how to get an accommodation if one was needed. Does this require new policies or new protocols during the interview phase?

Under the PWFA, employers cannot force an employee to take unpaid leave if other accommodations are available. Employers should, therefore, consider reassignment and other alternatives that would keep an employee on the job.

Although there are some limitations under the PWFA as to when and how an employer can ask for documentation, there will undoubtedly be situations where the requested accommodation is complex enough that seeking documentation from a healthcare provider makes sense. When those situations arise, the employer will need to draft a request that it uses solely for requests under the PWFA. In other words, employers should not use the same accommodation request form they use for FMLA or ADA situations.

*One final reminder:* Employers should always have job descriptions for each position that set out the essential functions. If they do not, it will be difficult to analyze which functions are essential and which ones are not. In the absence of a job description, it will be more difficult for an employer to argue that an accommodation constitutes an undue hardship.

This law is very new, and as is the case with any new law, employers should carefully monitor developments in the law and interpretations of the PWFA. In addition, employers should keep in mind that there is now EEOC guidance and a set of rules interpreting the Act that can be helpful and that can provide guidance when complex situations arise. Along these same lines, employers should be aware that state and local laws could provide further protections for employees than the protections provided by the PWFA.

CHAPTER 12

# Equal Pay Claims

Imagine this scenario: Due to a clerical error, for the past year, a male employee has been paid more than several females working in the very same position. The male was hired at about the same time as the females, has about the same level of education and experience, and largely performs at the same level as his female counterparts. The female employees recently found out about the pay disparity and have demanded that you immediately increase their pay so it is equal to the male's pay. They also demand that you issue them backpay to account for the pay differential from the time the male started to get paid more. You apologize profusely on behalf of the company. You then explain that this was an accident, there was no discrimination intended, and that your company cannot afford to write a large check to account for the difference. Surely, there cannot be an actionable claim based on a clerical error? Wrong.

Congress passed the Equal Pay Act (EPA) in 1963 with the goal of ending employment discrimination in private industry. Establishing a claim under the EPA is easy—a plaintiff must show only that the employer paid male and female employees different wages for substantially equal work. If an employee shows that (what we call a prima facie case), then the burden shifts to the employer to show that the wage disparity was, in fact, due to some reason other than the employee's gender. Under the Equal Pay Act, here are four explicit statutory exceptions: "(i) a seniority system; (ii) a merit system; (iii) a system which measures earnings by quantity or quality of production; or (iv) a differential based on any factor other than sex." All of these operate as affirmative defenses.

Many states have enacted state Equal Pay statutes that, in some cases, provide more protections for employees than the federal statute. Also, in cases where a pay disparity exists between males and females but where the jobs do not involve equal work, Title VII may also apply if the pay disparity can be traced to intentional discrimination.

These claims are high-risk for employers. If an employer has male employees being paid more than female employees performing the same job, it is, in many cases, easy for the females to prevail on the wage claim. Employers should take great measures to make sure they never end up in the situation described above. Equal pay claims are difficult to defend and can be extremely costly. Under the federal Equal Pay Act, a plaintiff can recover wages for a period of two years and get liquidated damages, i.e., double damages, unless the employer can show "good faith." While it seems like that would be easy, it is not—proving good faith is very difficult.

So, what should an employer be doing to avoid an Equal Pay claim? Keeping an eye on which jobs perform similar functions and keeping an eye on who is getting paid what should be a primary concern.

For example, if you have four engineers performing the same job, three of whom are male and one of whom is a woman, the presumption should be that they are all getting paid the same. If they are not, then some analysis is required. Are you able to explain how the pay differential was reached? In some cases, the answer might be no. Perhaps a former

HR professional approved the differential, and perhaps there is no documentation indicating how the decision was made. How was the pay difference reached, and what type of factors justify the spread? As is usually the case with employment law issues, you must be able to show that the business did what it did for legitimate, non-discriminatory reasons. The answer should always be yes.

Or imagine this scenario: What if your company hired a remote salesperson from a big city located out of state, where the job market demands higher salaries? If your company hired a male from out of state and paid him $10,000 per year more than the employees who were already performing that job, would that create a problem? Possibly. If the employees making the lower compensation are female, and if there is no other justification for the pay differential other than the fact that the male is in a different city, this type of scenario could lead to an Equal Pay claim.

Pay ranges, job descriptions, resumes, and job applications are all documents that can help with this analysis. Pay ranges can be a very effective way for an employer to group certain jobs together, figure out a range of compensation available, and ascertain what factors within those jobs warrant additional compensation. While creating a pay range scheme can be somewhat complex, when done properly, it can go a long way toward eliminating risk affiliated with equal pay claims and providing documentation needed to show that an employer's compensation decisions were based on legitimate, non-discriminatory reasons.

Job descriptions, resumes, and applications can also be effective for such an analysis, albeit on a somewhat less sophisticated level. If an employer can cite a job description that requires a certain level of experience, and if it can cite a resume or a job application to show that a male employee had ten years more experience than a female employee, then that could, in some cases, provide a legitimate, nondiscriminatory reason for a pay differential.

There are other ways an employer can avoid Equal Pay claims, too. However, the big take-away here is that we are operating in an ever-changing world where more and more employees work virtually and where more and more employers are hiring employees from other job markets. Thus, it makes sense to pay attention to the law and to understand that if you have employees performing similar work for different rates of pay, then it might raise questions, and you always need to be able to show that your compensation decisions are based on legitimate, non-discriminatory reasons (preferably reasons shown on available documentation).

# CHAPTER 13

# Retaliation

Tara had never been a strong performer. From the time she started in her role as a call center trainer, she had consistently failed to meet expectations. Robin, her supervisor, kept hoping she would see improvement, but it never really came. When the employer saw a downturn in revenue, it decided it would have to trim the payroll. In the context of that conversation, Tara's name was the one that always came up.

Robin had not done a great job of documenting Tara's deficiencies and lackluster performance but figured that there was little risk in moving forward with the termination. Unfortunately, Robin did not have any training on how to walk through a termination checklist, and she failed to realize that she should talk to the HR Director, Rachel, to analyze the risk before moving forward with the termination.

Had Robin followed a termination checklist, she would have learned from Rachel that Tara had spent quite a bit of time in the HR office during the past few months. Tara first approached Rachel four months ago and expressed concern that the employer was not following the law. Tara said that although she was classified as an exempt employee and did not qualify for overtime, she believed that, in reality, she was misclassified. She believed that she should be classified as a non-exempt employee and, thus, was owed back wages for overtime. Rachel had been buried with other emergencies, and up until one month ago, she had not had time to investigate Tara's complaint. However, Rachel had begun to dig into Tara's complaint, and Rachel had concluded that the answer was not clear-cut. Rachel thought that Tara's concerns were legitimate. While Rachel's investigation was ongoing, Tara was terminated by Robin.

In a different scenario, John worked as a mechanic at the local mechanic shop. As John rolled up on his one-year anniversary, he began to have serious safety concerns about the way his employer operated its business. John called OSHA and voiced his concerns. He then told his manager, Tim, that he had concerns and that he had reported the shop to OSHA. Tim fired John for insubordination.

In another example, Shane believed he was being harassed by Michelle on the basis of his LGBTQ+ status. He told Noel about his concerns, and she started a workplace investigation. Several weeks later, Shane's supervisor, Doug, told him that he was no longer a good fit for the company and terminated him.

Tara, Shane, and John could all possibly assert retaliation claims premised on the facts here. Some statutes, like Title VII and the Fair Labor Standards Act, expressly provide for a cause of action of retaliation if an employee seeks protection under the statute, as Tara and Shane did here, and is then terminated as a result. OSHA provides a similar remedy.

In some jurisdictions, there are also state statutes that provide additional protections from retaliation. For example, some states, like the one where I practice, provide whistleblower protections for public employees who get terminated for reporting legal violations, making allegations of public waste, or participating in an investigation, just to name a few scenarios.

In our state, there is likewise a common law claim called wrongful termination in violation of public policy that can give rise to retaliation claims. Imagine an employee who was injured in the workplace and then sought remedies under the worker's compensation statute. If the employee was then fired for taking advantage of statutorily provided remedies, that employee could assert a claim of wrongful termination in violation of public policy.

Basically, regardless of which statute or cause of action is at issue, an employee has to prove the same elements: that they engaged in protected activity, that they suffered an adverse action, and that there is a causal connection between the adverse action and the protected activity. In order to avoid such claims, employers should be aware of the following types of conduct that can qualify as "protected activity" and that can trigger a claim:

- Participation in any type of investigation

- Complaints of discrimination and/or harassment

- Safety complaints/OSHA

- Complaints of internal fraud/waste/unlawful activity

- An ADA request for accommodation

- Filing for worker's compensation benefits

All of these, and others like them, can raise the issue of possible retaliation, and employers need good policies and processes—and training—to flag the issue before they take action that could result in a claim.

## CHAPTER 14

# Wage and Hour Issues—
# Contributing Author Benjamin T. Cramer

Wait—don't go! I know you may be tempted to skip to the next chapter, and maybe your eyes glazed over a bit when you read the title. But I promise to do my best to make this interesting. The reality is that wage and hour issues are a place that trips up a number of leaders—from small businesses to large-scale corporations. And while the facts and circumstances around these cases may not be as intriguing as some of the other areas of this book, the consequences are often incredibly costly for employers. Wage claims under Federal law come with a two- or three-year statute of limitations, along with the presumption of liquidated (double) damages and likely civil money penalties. States may have further penalties. In addition, the US Department of Labor (DOL)—the federal agency in charge of enforcing the Fair Labor Standards Act (FLSA)—also puts out a press release highlighting their enforcement success, potentially damaging your company's reputation. All that to say, it's worth it—both financially and reputationally—to think through wage issues.

From my experience, very few leaders have thought through their wage and hour policies—everything from "Is this person an employee?" and "Are they paid correctly?" to "What do I do if a DOL Wage and Hour Division Investigator waltzes in the front door and starts speaking with employees?" I hear a range of explanations, from: "This is how the industry does it" to "My employees and I created this arrangement, and they are happy." Unfortunately, while these may be true, that does not mean the arrangements are compliant with the law. I also hear, "We're a small business that only operates in our state, so we just have to comply with state law." That's most likely not the case, as the jurisdiction of the Fair Labor Standards Act applies to most businesses that have two employees and an annual gross sales volume of $500,000 per year. In addition, even if your business is not covered as a whole, certain employees may be covered based on job duties that cross state lines. Finally, interrelated businesses with common ownership or shared employees are often considered one business for the purposes of determining coverage under the FLSA.

Now that I've got your attention, let's briefly walk through the things that a leader needs to be cognizant of in relation to wage and hour issues. Here are a couple of quick caveats: This chapter is going to focus on the federal Fair Labor Standards Act (FLSA). As I just mentioned, most businesses are covered by the FLSA based on the volume of gross sales they make in a year. However, there may also be more restrictive state laws in play, so it's good to speak with a state-specific wage and hour attorney. Second, there's a lot of nuance when it comes to understanding and interpreting regulations. The goal of this chapter is to help you spot potential issues, which should then be vetted by a wage and hour attorney in your state. Often, the Wage and Hour Division will also be willing to provide training and answers regarding compliance, and their training and investigations units are typically separated—meaning questions to the training unit should not result in an investigation.

With those caveats in mind, let's dive into the top issues that leaders need to be aware of.

## Independent Contractor vs. Employee

One of the first major issues is whether a person doing work for a business is an independent contractor or an employee. First, as a leader, you need to know that if you want someone to be an "employee" and subject to the FLSA (and other laws that may be applicable to the employee/employer relationship), then that's fine. You can typically define someone who may otherwise meet the definition of an independent contractor as an employee without issue. However, there are some advantages for a worker to be an independent contractor—both for the worker and company. These can include tax benefits, independence, and issues related to benefits and insurance. Independent Contractors are also not generally covered by the FLSA regulations and other state and federal laws governing the employee/employer relationship, including Title VII and the ADA.

Over the past couple of decades, there has been a bit of a ping-pong match regarding the "test" that the Wage and Hour Division will use to determine whether an individual is an independent contractor or employee. Some of this was a result of the development of the gig economy and unique questions that surfaced, but it was also heavily influenced by the changes in presidential administrations. In 2024, for the purposes of the Fair Labor Standards Act, a test called the "Economic Reality Test" was enacted to guide the independent contractor vs. employee analysis. At its heart, the fundamental question is to determine whether the employee is economically dependent on the employer for work or, alternatively, is in business for themselves. Six typical factors are identified—none of which are weighted more heavily or dispositive in-and-of themselves. In addition, the test notes that "additional factors" may also be relevant and considered. Ultimately, it all comes down to the "economic reality" based on the totality of the circumstances. Here are those six factors:

1.  Opportunity for profit or loss depending on managerial skill

2.  Investments by the workers and the employer

3.  Permanence of the working relationship

4.  Nature and degree of control

5.  Whether the work performed is integral to the employer's business

6.  Skill and initiative

If you want to learn more about each of these, the U.S. Department of Labor Wage and Hour Division publishes guidance and hypotheticals for each of these factors. But, as you can imagine, the hypotheticals offered are at the far extremes of each of these factors, and leaders almost always operate in the "gray" area.

That brings me to the most important point for a leader: You need to be aware of these factors, and you need to know what can cause a factor to tip in one direction or another. If you want a contractor to use a company computer or software, that may be fine...but it tips the "investment" factor toward employer-provided investment rather than worker investment. If you want to require the worker to be on site from 8 am to noon, to provide frequent oversight on a project done by the worker, or to provide a performance evaluation for the worker, there may be paths to do each of these, but you need to know that they tip the "nature and degree of control" into more of an employee/employer relationship rather than a contractor relationship. In short, small changes in how you oversee what you intend to be a contractor can have appreciable impacts on whether the individual is actually a contractor under this test.

One other major point that a leader needs to be aware of: You'll notice the test is the "economic realities test" that is based on the "totality of circumstances" of six typical factors, though additional factors may be considered. I hope you noticed that this is a highly subjective test, and sometimes a factor that seems very dispositive to you may not carry the same weight with the investigator or judge assigned to the claim. To the greatest extent possible, it's best to have as many factors weighing toward "independent contractor" if that's your preferred relationship. Finally, as noted above, the test used for independent contractors has undergone a number of changes over the last 20 years, primarily based on a change in the presidential administrations. So, it's important to stay up to date—and re-evaluate each contractor—based on the currently existing test.

## Exempt Employees

"They are paid a salary, so they are exempt." I can't understate the number of times that I've heard this statement from a leader. And, similar to a childhood math problem, while the answer may be right, it's important to show your work on how you arrived at the solution. But, from a fundamental standpoint, paying someone a salary **does not make them exempt.**

First, let's briefly discuss what we mean by "exempt." There are two aspects of the Fair Labor Standards Act that we are typically referring to when we discuss "exempt"—minimum wage and maximum hours (aka overtime). Importantly, there are some situations where an employee may be exempt from one but not the other. However, typically, we are talking about employees being exempt from both.

*Here's what is important:* When we're talking about employees who are NOT exempt from minimum wage OR overtime, an employer has a responsibility to ensure that an employee's hours worked are accurately tracked. Further, it's necessary to track hours worked to determine whether the wages paid to the employee are sufficient to cover minimum wage and, likewise, to determine the overtime premium wage that must be paid to the employee for any hours worked over 40 in a workweek (under Federal law—again, some states may be even more restrictive).

In order to be exempt for either overtime, minimum wage, or both, most exemptions require an employee to be paid on what's called a "salary basis." But this is only the first step in determining an exemption. The second step is that an employee's job duties must align with the "duties test" of one of the exemptions.

So, if you take nothing else from this subsection, as a leader, you need to stop saying, "They are paid a salary, so they're exempt." Instead, you need to start saying, "They are paid a salary, and their duties align with an exemption, so they are exempt from minimum wage, overtime, or both."

Similar to the independent contractor vs. employee question, there used to be a "presumption" that an employee was a non-exempt employee unless the employer could definitively show the employee met the requirements of an exemption. But that's no longer the case—and, again, there's an equal playing field where the investigator or a court will determine whether an employee qualifies for an exemption.

While there are some more nuanced exemptions that may be applicable based on specific industries (seasonal amusement and recreational establishments, car repair shops, transportation, farmworkers, fishing, academia, hospitals, and residential care facilities, etc.), the more typical exemptions are frequently referred to as the "White Collar Exemptions." These include the Executive Exemption, the Administrative Exemption, and the Professional Exemption.

Let's briefly touch on each of these:

### *Executive Exemption:*

Requires payment on a salary basis. Their primary duty must be managing either the enterprise in which the person is employed or a customarily recognized department or subdivision of the enterprise. As a part of that management, they must regularly direct the work of at least two or more full-time employees or the equivalent. Finally, in their direction of the employees, they must have the authority to hire and fire the employees, or their recommendations must be given weight.

## Administrative Exemption:

Requires payment on a salary basis. In addition, their primary duty must be the performance of non-manual work that is directly related to the management or general business operations of the employer, and, with respect to their primary duty, they exercise discretion and independent judgment with respect to matters of significance.

## Professional Exemption:

There are actually a few subgroups under the professional exemption, which complicates things a bit.

- **Learned Professional:** Requires payment on a salary basis. Their primary duty must be the performance of work requiring advanced knowledge that is predominantly intellectual and requires the consistent exercise of discretion and judgment. The advanced knowledge must be in a field of science or learning and must be customarily required by a prolonged course of study. Put differently, these are typically primary duties that require a Master's or Doctorate degree.

- **Creative Professional:** Requires payment on a salary basis. Their primary duty must be the performance of work requiring invention, imagination, originality, or talent in a recognized field of artistic or creative endeavor. Some examples include music, writing, acting, and graphic arts.

- **Lawyers and Doctors:** All this requires is that the person holds a valid license and is actively practicing law or medicine. If that's the case, they're exempt from both minimum wage and overtime. There is no salary basis requirement.

- **Teachers:** There is also no salary basis requirement for teachers. As long as a person's primary duty is teaching, tutoring, instructing, or lecturing in the activity of imparting knowledge, and they are employed and engaged in this activity as a teacher in an educational establishment, they are exempt from both overtime and minimum wage.

  You might have been tracking with me right up until teachers. Is there no salary, minimum wage, or overtime premium required for teachers? Not under Federal law.

There are a few other exemptions regarding sales—namely the outside sales and inside sales exemptions. Those are more nuanced, but roughly speaking, think of outside sales as a traditional traveling salesperson who is visiting customer locations. Inside sales is anyone based at a location (including folks primarily telecommuting from home selling for a business). Inside sales can only be exempt from overtime, not minimum wage. The outside sales exemption can apply to both.

### Highly Compensated Employee Exemption:

Finally, there is the **Highly Compensated Employee** exemption. The key here is that an employee must be paid on a salary basis, have a primary duty that includes office or non-manual work, customarily or regularly perform at least one of the exempt duties of an executive, administrative, or provisional employee, AND over the course of the year, earn a salary that is currently $107,432, although there are ongoing attempts to increase this amount. I can't overemphasize how important it is to make sure that each factor is satisfied—not just the total compensation—before assuming that this exemption will apply. In a recent United States Supreme Court case, *Helix Energy Solutions v. Hewitt,* an off-shore oil rig manager was paid a daily rate of more than $963, performed at least one executive duty, and made more than $200,000 a year, but still was deemed to be a non-exempt employee because his compensation structure did not properly comport with the salary basis test—an incredibly costly error considering he routinely worked 12 hours a day for 28 consecutive days.

You probably noted that there are two frequent terms bandied about in relation to exemptions—paid on a salary basis and primary duty. Let's look at both of those.

## Paid on a Salary Basis

What does it mean to be paid on a salary basis? From a foundational standpoint, it's important to understand that salary is discussed in terms of each workweek, which is a 7-day or 168-hour period. If no work is performed in that workweek, no salary is due.

Beyond that, for an exemption to apply, there's a minimum dollar amount that must be paid. This amount is paid for any work done during the workweek, and unless there's a specific permissible deduction, it needs to be paid whether the person did a minuscule amount of work for the workweek or a ton of work. Currently, the salary amount must be greater than or equal to $684 per week. Like the Highly Compensated employee number, there are attempts to increase this amount that – at the time of publication – are currently being litigated.

In addition to the amount, a salary payment is required regardless of the amount of work performed during the workweek. As a leader, if you pay someone a salary, I want you to think twice ANY TIME you're about to reduce a salaried employee's weekly pay because they didn't work as much as you hoped or anticipated. If a salaried employee works at all during a workweek, then your default should be they receive the full salary for that week.

Now, there are some limited times when it is okay to reduce someone's salary in a week they did work. For instance, it's permissible to deduct **full days** when it's an employee's first or last week of work (pay them only for the days worked) when they take a personal day other than for sickness or disability, or if you have a *bona fide* sick leave plan and they have used up all their sick leave hours, then you can typically reduce any time they don't work the **entire day.** In contrast, there are very few times when it's permissible to deduct a **partial day.** As a leader, you need to know that a partial day deduction is rarely permitted.

Finally, you can never reduce an employee's salary when the employee is available to work but unable to do so because of the employer, court service, or military service. So, if you close the business for a holiday or inclement weather on a couple of days during the workweek, you can't deduct that closure from an employee's salary. If you tell an employee to use their vacation time to cover closure on a holiday and they don't have any, you can't deduct that closure. If an employee is required to serve on a jury, appear as a witness, or perform a temporary military duty, you also can't deduct the employee's salary for the days in the workweek not worked. Again, if these things result in the employee performing no work during the entire workweek, then that's likely different.

Ultimately, be cautious any time that you are deducting from a salary, and make sure it's a permissible deduction. The consequences of not doing so can be disastrous. If found to have made impermissible deductions, it can eliminate the exemption and result in a recalculation of the wages owed going back two or three years, plus liquidated (double) damages and civil money penalties. To avoid some of these potential consequences, you should ensure your handbook has a "Safe Harbor Provision" that explains when deductions are permitted, that the employer only takes permissible deductions, and how an employee should question or correct any issues with potentially impermissible deductions. This can help ensure that a mistaken impermissible deduction doesn't completely eliminate the exemption.

## Primary Duty

Primary duty is another term frequently used when discussing exemptions. This term is defined in the regulations as "the principal, main, major, or most important duty that the employee performs" (29 CFR 541.700). This doesn't mean that it's the duty that takes up the most time, but it does need to be the main or most important duty of the role. Once you've identified the primary duty, you can analyze whether it would meet the qualifications of one or more of the exemptions above.

## Wrapping up Exempt Employees

We're about to turn to non-exempt employees. But, before we do, I wanted to hit just a couple of the important key things for a leader. First, make sure you know what you mean by an "exempt" employee—are we talking exempt from overtime, minimum wage, or both? Second, make sure you've evaluated all the factors of the exemption you are claiming for the position. Third, be cautious anytime you're reducing an exempt employee's salary. Finally, these are nuanced issues, and it's important to seek legal advice when evaluating exemptions and deductions. In some instances, a letter from an attorney advising you in a certain way can provide a "good faith" defense in any further investigations or litigation. That won't absolve you from paying the back wages due, but it can protect you from the doubling of those damages (liquidated damages).

## Non-Exempt Employees and Pay Structures

Now that we've discussed exempt employees, let's look at non-exempt employees. These are employees who are owed at least minimum wage for every hour worked and are also required to be paid overtime for any hours worked over 40 in a workweek. The current federal minimum wage (at the time of publishing) for most workers is $7.25 per hour, though there are some federal contractor rules that can increase this minimum. Similarly, certain states and localities have increased minimum wages.

The U.S. Department of Labor will enforce state laws that are more restrictive than federal law.

My sense is that most leaders understand how hourly employees are typically paid. First, an employer defines a workweek as a set 7-day, 168-hour period. In most circumstances, this workweek will not and should not change. Employees who work more than 40 hours in the workweek are due an overtime premium for any hours worked beyond 40. This means that those hours are paid at "time and a half." Federally, there are no daily overtime rates, though some states have enacted rules that require overtime payments when an employee's daily work crosses a certain threshold, such as 8 hours.

The biggest issues that leaders miss when it comes to non-exempt employees typically involve the calculation of an employee's "regular rate," tracking an employee's hours for multiple positions separately, declining to pay employees for unauthorized overtime, telling employees to go home early next week to make up for extra hours this week, and failing to ensure employees properly track and report their hours.

### Forms of Payment for Hourly Employees

Employers may be surprised to learn that there are various ways that an employee can be compensated even when not exempt from overtime and/or minimum wage. These include the traditional "hourly" wage but also include things like a weekly salary, piece rate (per piece produced), and commissions. There are various rules that apply to each of these, and, in cases like a weekly salary, there must be a clear written understanding of how many hours that weekly salary contemplates, but employers may have more options than they realize when it comes to paying non-exempt employees.

That said, at the end of the day, regardless of how a non-exempt employee is paid, the employer must make sure that the employee is receiving at least the applicable minimum wage and the overtime premium wage for any hours over 40 in the workweek. The key to this calculation is determining the regular rate.

## Regular Rate

The regular rate is calculated for each workweek. Depending on the pay structure, it can fluctuate each work week. This is the rate on which 1) confirmation that the employee has made minimum wage occurs, and 2) calculation of the overtime premium is based. For a traditional hourly employee, this is easy. Take the following example:

> An employee makes $20 per hour and works 30 hours per week. The employee is paid a regular rate of $20 per hour.

Where things can get more complicated is when piece rate, salary, commissions, or split roles are involved.

For instance, take the same hourly employee. For 30 hours in the workweek, that employee worked as a restaurant host at a rate of $10 per hour. For 10 hours of that same workweek, the employee worked as a bookkeeper for the business at a rate of $30 per hour. Here, the employee's regular rate is $15.00:

$$((30 \text{ hrs.} * \$10) + (10 \text{ hrs.} * \$30)) / (30 \text{ hrs.} + 10 \text{ hrs.}) = \text{Regular Rate of } \$15$$

In this instance, the employee's regular rate is $15.00, which is above the federal minimum wage. The total wages earned for the period is $600.

Let's complicate this further. Using the same example, let's assume that the employee works 10 hours as a bookkeeper at the start of the week. The employee then is scheduled for 30 hours for the remainder of the week as a host. However, the employee picks up a shift and ends up working 35 hours as a host. Leaders are sometimes tempted to say that the overtime rate is consistent with the wage rate of the position that the overtime occurred in and that's partially correct. But the overtime premium (the "half" of the "time and a half") is paid out based on the regular rate. So, here's the calculation in this scenario:

((10 hrs. * $30) + (35 hrs. * $10)) / (10 hrs. + 35 hrs.) = Regular Rate of $14.44

The overtime hours worked in this scenario are 5 hours. So, the wages due are:

10 hours * $30 = $300

35 hours * $10 = $350

Overtime Premium: 5 hrs. * ($14.44 Regular Rate / 2) = $36.10

If you had paid the 5 overtime hours out at $15.00 ($10 x 1.5), you would have underpaid this employee by $11.10 for this workweek. The correct premium wage for each of those hours was $17.22 ($10 + ($14.44 / 2). Under the FLSA, the employee would be entitled to liquidated damages for this underpayment, meaning that this will be doubled, and $22.20 would be the damages. Now, go back through every incorrect rate for the last two, possibly three years for every employee, and you start to see how wage recovery in these types of actions easily ranges from the five to seven figures for employers, even before the penalties.

Perhaps math is not your strong suit, and that's fine. The big takeaway here is that finding the regular rate is not always easy.

This can be further complicated when using salary payments for non-exempt employees, fluctuating workweek methods, commissions, or piece rate methods. It's important that leaders understand that these issues can be complicated and ensure that proper guidance is obtained when calculating overtime wages and ensuring compliance with minimum wage rules.

## *Tip Credit vs. Tip Pooling*

A quick note regarding tip credits and tip pooling. If you're in an industry where employees regularly receive tips, it may be possible to take a "tip credit." Roughly speaking, this allows a portion of tips to cover a portion of minimum wage, resulting in a lower minimum wage owed by the employer. However, tip credits are heavily regulated, and failure to strictly comply with the rules will be costly. If you're considering a tip credit—paying a minimum wage lower than $7.25—make sure you get competent legal advice on your tipping structure BEFORE you implement it.

There is a distinction between taking a "tip credit" and having a "tipping pool"—though there are regulations around both. Tip pooling is the employer-facilitated sharing of tips. Before a tip pool is implemented, it is important to consult a wage and hour attorney. Because tips are generally presumed to be intended for the person who received them—and them alone—there are rules and limitations regarding employer-facilitated tip pools.

Incorrect tip credits and tip pools are a huge area of emphasis for the Wage and Hour Division. On a daily basis, restaurants across the country are found to be non-compliant, typically to the tune of at least $100,000 in back wages owed. It may seem objectively fair to require a server to share tips with the host, busser, dishwasher, or kitchen staff—all of whom are likely instrumental to the customer's overall experience—but there are strict, nuanced guidelines that must be followed to do so. The consequences of failing to do so are incredibly costly (double damages, a look-back period of three years, and civil money penalties). Even worse, if an employer (including an agent of the employer like a manager, assistant manager, or supervisor) impermissibly retains tips and is taking the tip credit, the employer may face retroactive loss of the tip credit AND the requirement to reimburse tips, doubled, for three years, plus civil money penalties.

I routinely assist restaurants through this process and empathize with my clients whose servers were taking home really good money despite being required to share a small percentage of their tips. But, at the end of the day, it doesn't matter whether the servers were "well paid" and "felt taken care of"—it only matters whether the pay structure complies with the law. One curious random Wage and Hour Investigator—or one former disgruntled employee complaint—can kick the door open for an investigation of the entire business. Once an investigation starts, it doesn't matter if the vast majority of folks were good with the pay structure—the wages and damages will still be owed to employees regardless of whether they think the employer did anything wrong.

### Non-Discretionary Bonus/Commissions vs. Discretionary Bonuses

Leaders need to know that non-discretionary bonuses and commissions impact an employee's regular rate. As a result, if the employee had overtime paid out during the same period that the commission or non-discretionary bonus was for, then there likely will be an overtime premium that is also due on top of the commission or non-discretionary bonus. This is because those are anticipated forms of compensation for the hours when the hours were worked. Leaders need to be aware of this when considering whether to enact a commission structure or a non-discretionary bonus structure involving non-exempt employees.

Conversely, a truly discretionary bonus is not part of a non-exempt employee's regular rate. The discretionary nature means that an employee could not have expected it to be paid out, and therefore, it is not part of their wages for the hours worked.

### Recordkeeping

For non-exempt employees, there are a number of records that must be maintained by employers. This includes the agreed-upon wage rate, timesheets, and pay stubs for the last three years. As demonstrated above, these are critical to being able to calculate the wages owed and prove that an employee was properly paid. Leaders need to be aware of their recordkeeping obligations and ensure compliance.

## Technology and Time Reporting

An emerging issue that leaders need to be aware of involves the reporting of time and technology. An employer is expected to ensure that its employees are accurately tracking time, and if an employer knows or should have known that an employee didn't properly record their time, then they need to ensure it is done correctly.

Leaders should make sure that employees know that no off-the-clock work is permitted. In addition, in the age of technology and timestamps, leaders need to make sure that any work that employees perform is reported consistently with the time actually worked. For example, if a non-exempt employee responds to a work-related email or text message at 10:45 pm, then the leader needs to make sure that the employee's timecard reflects that they worked at 10:45 pm. If it doesn't, then there's a clear digital trail that the employee is performing work and not receiving compensation for that time, and it will be hard for an employer to justify that they didn't know about the work performed.

## Withholding Wages

As I mentioned earlier, two other things I often encounter with leaders are:

1. telling employees they will not pay them for unauthorized overtime, and

2. telling employees to move their extra time from one workweek to the next workweek—or giving some other compensatory time (extra vacation, etc.).

Outside of public employers, there is no such thing as compensatory time for non-exempt employees. If an employee works more than 40 hours in a workweek, they must be paid the overtime wage and premium for those hours. It can't be comped or otherwise made up in the following week. Leaders need to make sure that employees are accurately tracking and reporting the time worked.

Similarly, if work is performed on behalf of an employer, it must be compensated. This is true even if an employee works unauthorized overtime. In those instances, the employer must pay. The employer's recourse is disciplinary action toward the employee for failing to follow employer policies.

## Child Labor

The FLSA also covers child labor. If you're contemplating hiring or employing individuals who are 17 years old or under, it's incredibly important that you know and understand the rules around child labor. The number one area I see that trips up leaders is when they hire their own child or allow an employee to have their child work for the business. While there are some deviations for agriculture and when the child's parents are the sole owner of the business, in the vast majority of circumstances, the child labor rules apply. That means no employment under 14 years of age, strict rules for 14-15 year olds, and enhanced rules for 16-17 year olds.

This is another area that the Wage and Hour Division takes a keen interest in. It's also one of the areas where no benefit is received by the employee/child for the investigation—the civil money penalties all go to the division. Also, similar to all other areas of the FLSA, there is little deference to the "spirit" of the law over the letter of the law. Most of us can imagine "hazardous" occupations—and for 80% of them, you'd either be able to guess them yourself or kick yourself for not getting it right. Mining, millwork, manufacturing—those seem routine. Where people get surprised are some of the age-dependent prohibitions on ladders (including footstools or stepladders over two steps), loading and assisting around a vehicle, any baking activities (including preparation of pizzas), and lawn mowers. (Now think, when did you have your first lawn mowing job?) There are also strict age-dependent hour requirements not only during school weeks but also between June 1 and Labor Day. Each of these violations carries with it a $15,000+ penalty per violation per child, so if one 15-year-old child violated work hours and also used a ladder, then that's a $30,000 penalty right out of the gate.

The biggest issue I typically see is a manager or supervisor allowing their under-14-year-old child to work for the business, either cleaning the office, mowing the lawn, picking up the mail, or bussing a table. These all may be tasks that a child may have been doing around the house since they were 9 years old. But, unless the business is wholly owned by parents, no employees under 14 years of age are allowed. This includes a child volunteering to help—the employer has an obligation to stop them from doing the work, even if it did not affirmatively authorize them to do so to begin with.

## Preparing for a Wage and Hour Investigation

Beyond ensuring that their policies and procedures are in place, leaders should also put a plan in place for a Wage and Hour Investigation. While the practice varies from region to region, typically, a Wage and Hour Investigator will arrive at a company's door, show their credentials, demand to see pay records, and start talking with employees and managers on duty. Often, investigators try to time their investigations for when the owner or primary leadership is not in the office.

The investigators are skilled at their jobs. They are often kind to employees and low-level managers and ask general questions about their jobs, duties, if they receive tips, etc. During these conversations, they are listening for potential violations—how tips are shared, if a child has ever done work in the building, how time is tracked, how payroll is processed, etc. If there's been a prior complaint, they will often have an idea of which employees may be the best sources of information and which managers would be best to speak with.

While the best practice is often to comply and work with the investigators, it is always prudent to have a plan in place for responding to investigators. Again, the investigator coming in is very prepared, and though you might not have been expecting them that day, you should be prepared as well.

Ideally, when an investigator arrives, they will be shown to a conference room while leadership and legal counsel are contacted. The investigator may insist that they speak with employees immediately, but it's perfectly reasonable for a front desk employee to say that they don't have the authority to assist with the investigator's request and that they'll contact the person with authority. There is some reasonable latitude for the employer to work with the investigator on scheduling interviews to minimize the impact on business operations. The employer also can and should let employees know about the investigation and that they have the right to participate (or not participate)—the choice is entirely theirs. Employers should also encourage employees to be truthful in their responses if they choose to participate and make it clear that no retaliation will occur for their participation or non-participation in the investigation. The employee can also elect to have a member of management sit in the interview with them.

When it comes to managers/supervisors, it is the employer's choice as to whether or not to have a representative in the room when the conversation is occurring. Leaders should instruct their managers/ supervisors to have legal counsel or a leader who understands the wage and hour rules to be present any time that manager/supervisor speaks with the investigator. As an agent of the employer, anything that the manager/supervisor says to the investigator will be taken as though the employer said it. To that end, I can't tell you the number of times that a manager has shared an incorrect perspective of how things work, only for the employer to have to unwind those statements based on the actual facts, policies, and documents. It is much better for the investigator's first impression to be an accurate one than it is to have to walk back inaccurate impressions conveyed by managers/supervisors.

At the end of the day, as the old adage says, "An ounce of prevention is worth a pound of cure." A leader who ensures they are compliant with all facets of the FLSA, who ensures routine audits of their processes, who ensures the correct records are being maintained, who is aware of the boundaries and what factors can change the analysis, and who ensures their employees and teams know, understand, and are following their processes, will be just fine in any wage and hour investigation. But, it's always helpful to have a plan for when the investigator walks through the door—a plan to ensure they are getting helpful, accurate information with minimal disruption to your business.

## Key Takeaways:

- If your organization has independent contractors, you need to be aware of the Economic Realities Test and the factors that are used to determine whether a contractor is actually an employee. Relatedly, you also need to be cognizant of the slightly different tests used by the IRS and the state(s) in which you are operating for programs like unemployment insurance/benefits and worker's compensation. Changes in how you interact with your independent contractors—such as when they need to be available to perform work, the requirement that they use your software/systems, or a new expectation that they perform work exclusively for you—could impact the analysis. At the end of the day, you want to ensure your independent contractors are as solidly within as many factors as possible.

- Leaders should make sure that they conduct a routine analysis of exempt employees to ensure they still qualify for an exemption from overtime and/or minimum wage. What exemptions are we talking about for this employee? Have their duties changed? Does their salary still qualify? What is the basis for the exemption? Are they conducting two or more positions where, in aggregate, they are no longer exempt? For employees who are close to the line, it may be prudent to have a "good faith" letter from an attorney to rely upon should the employee ultimately be found to be non-exempt.

- Leaders should think twice before making any deductions from a salaried employee's weekly salary for any week in which they performed work. Full-day deductions can only be made in limited circumstances, and partial-day deductions are almost never allowed. A "safe harbor" provision should also be in an employer's handbook to help prevent mistakes from inadvertently converting an exempt employee to a non-exempt employee due to the overtime premium.

- Leaders should make sure that they are accurately tracking hours for non-exempt employees. While you can make it your employee's responsibility to track their own hours, the company (and its leaders) are ultimately responsible for ensuring that the correct hours are reported. With the increased sophistication of time clocks and tracking of specific hours worked, combined with the timestamps on emails and text messages, leaders should make sure that the reported hours worked align with the timestamps of work performed by employees.

- Leaders should be cautious any time they are using or redirecting a portion of an employee's tips. Tips are considered the employee's money, and the regulations around tip-pooling, tip-sharing, and using tips to make up a portion of wages are very strict. These areas of the law are rife with tripping hazards and require strict adherence. Frankly, many of the "standard practices" in the tipping professions that I hear about are problematic. In short, this is an area where legal advice is strongly advised and far more reliable than how the competitor down the street is doing it.

- Leaders need to make sure to flag off-the-clock work- and pay the time actually worked—and then discipline employees who failed to report time actually worked. It is essential that employees do effective, accurate time tracking and that a leader takes the time to verify it (e.g., cross reference with the first and last emails/texts you got from that employee on the given day).

- Leaders need to be very aware of the restrictions related to the employment of individuals who are 17 years of age or under, even if it's their own child.

# CHAPTER 15

# Keeping Your Information Safe— Contributing Author Doug Plass

It is an old story. An employer brings on a new employee. Things are going well, and the employer allows the employee more and more responsibility and access to important information. And then, the relationship sours unexpectedly. The employee leaves and takes with him proprietary information, customer lists, and basically the employer's entire playbook. The employer is left wondering what happened, does not know how to respond, is nervous about being burned again in the future, and is forced to reevaluate how the business is run.

One caveat to this section is that these issues tend to be a matter of state law. This chapter focuses on high-level concepts and, to some degree, my experience in the state where I live. However, it is not an overview of state law, and you should learn the law in your state. It will be well worth your time, as the issue comes up more than you might think.

Take Sage, for example. Sage owned a business that manufactured and sold some specialty electronic components. Because Sage's business started small and because she had always been able to work out issues with her employees fairly, Sage did not bother creating an employee handbook or having her employees enter into any agreements with the business. Dana came to work for Sage as a salesperson and, after years with the company, was put in charge of the entire sales force. Without warning, Dana left. Although it was difficult to adapt to the loss of this key employee, Sage was able to promote another employee into Dana's former role and move forward. Some weeks later, Sage's new sales manager received an email from a client inquiring about a shipment. After a bit of confusion, Sage discovered that the client was asking about a purchase from a competitor of Sage's business that Dana had gone to work for and had reached out to Sage's business by mistake. This caused Sage to take a look at Dana's old email account, where it was discovered that Dana had emailed a number of Sage's files to a personal email address, including her customer list, customer buying history, and internal business processes. Sage was left dumbfounded by what had occurred and did not know how she had gotten to this point. Had Sage taken some time to plan for the protection of her confidential information and her business' interests going forward, she could have either avoided this situation entirely or had a number of remedies available to her to deal with it.

Employment relationships are tricky. Employers need to be able to give employees the freedom to do their jobs, but with that freedom comes opportunities to do things that are not in the employer's interest. Employers must invest in their employees to get the most out of them, but those investments can be lost when the employee leaves or, worse, can be used to actively work against the employer's business. Employees represent their employers in dealings with customers and vendors, but in doing so, they create relationships that can be leveraged by the employee after leaving. Employers need employees to access and use confidential information and trade secrets to do their jobs, but they also need to make sure that that information is not used for other purposes. To address this tension and these challenges, employers need to be aware of where things can go wrong and use the tools available to them to prevent and prepare for situations where current and/or former employees are not acting with the employer's best interests at heart.

Initially, employers should start by figuring out what information they have. This may seem like a simple step, but often, employers will not even consider that information ought to be protected. Employers may want to ask the following questions:

1.  What is the information that we created that we need to operate our business?

2.  What processes or practices have we developed over time that are unique to us (even if they have not been collected together in some document)?

3.  What kinds of information do we compile that is of particular use to us and could be valuable to a competitor, such as customer lists and the history of what we sold or produced for our customers?

4.  What information do we collect from our customers and employees that is either protected by law or that they might want to see protected?

Once an employer knows what the collection of information that it may want to protect is, it should ask itself whether all of this information is really necessary to run its business. For example, if a company has collected something like the social security numbers of its customers, ask whether there is a reason to have that information in the first place or any situation in which the business could legitimately use it. If the answer is "no," confidential information of third parties should be returned and/or purged from the business files. When someone's confidential information is acquired, the duty to protect it often comes along with it. It is a bad idea for a business to expose itself to potential liability unnecessarily.

Also, there may be information found within the company's files that was considered confidential at one time but is now really not protectable. This may involve processes, for instance, that have become commonly known through the passage of time or that really do not have any use in current situations or future possibilities. Businesses should not waste their time and effort trying to protect something that they have no use for. Indeed, when those sensitive secret things are interspersed with easily accessible public information, it makes it harder than it should be to identify what is really important.

In short, knowing what you have, why you have it, and what harm would occur if it was disclosed to others is an essential step in safeguarding protectable information.

## Workplace Policies

Once you know what information you want to protect, you will then want to create systems to do just that. A good place to start is with workplace policies. These lay out ways of doing things for everyone to follow so that all members of your organization know what is expected of them and what they should expect of each other.

Within policies, a business may consider requiring that its sensitive information not leave its control by requiring that it be kept in a secure location, both virtually and physically. For instance, a business may prohibit employees from linking to its file system from their personal devices. Or a business could require that sensitive physical files be kept in a locked room. Or it could restrict employees' ability to access its information from remote locations or make sure that whenever they do, it is in a secure manner protected from being intercepted. Indeed, the more sensitive the information, the greater the lengths employers may want to go to create systems that ensure its protection. For the most sensitive documents, an employer may want to require that access be logged such that it can determine who had access and when that access occurred.

Often, employers will benefit by issuing electronic devices to their employees that they can use to access the employers' systems. However, when the employment relationship is terminated, there are often situations where those employer devices remain in the employees' possession for some period of time, or the employer may not be able to get the devices back at all. This potentially puts a large amount of information at risk. Employers that have the ability to remotely disable their devices may be able to deal with situations where they are unable to retrieve them. Employers may want to have their employees surrender the employer devices for inspection and install the latest software periodically. This could detect any potential problems with the disclosure of confidential information and ensure that the employer is well set up to deal with a departing employee.

In the modern world, personal devices are ubiquitous. Employers may not even think twice about having an employee use their own device for work. After all, no one wants to carry two cell phones. If an employer is to allow such things, it should, through its policies, specify exactly how personal devices can or should be used. It should spell out what of its information can be stored on these employee devices and develop a clear procedure for ensuring that protected information is not put there to begin with, or if it is allowed, that it is removed in a way that satisfies the employer's security concerns.

## Confidentiality and Non-Disclosure Agreements

A key way that businesses can protect their information is through the use of confidentiality or non-disclosure agreements. These are agreements where the employee promises not to take or share the employer's protected information, and are effective when properly used, to both put employees on notice of what behavior is expected of them and also to give employers a way to respond if employees or former employees do not live up to their end of the bargain. If an employer has a legally binding agreement in place, and it discovers that an employee has taken or shared information in violation of the agreement, often, simply pointing out to the employee what their obligations are is enough to stop the offending behavior.

Employers should be cautioned, however, to avoid trying to protect information when they are not legally entitled to do so. By doing so, they run the risk that a court could throw out an entire confidentiality agreement because it goes too far. An example of this is information having to do with an employee's compensation. Employers cannot completely restrict their employees from discussing their own pay. If they do, it will be seen as an action interfering with employees' ability to organize and advocate under the National Labor Relations Act.

There are times when the business needs to share its confidential and even trade secret information with third parties. A Non-Disclosure Agreement (NDA) may be extremely helpful in these situations as a business will be able to create a legally binding obligation on the part of the third party to protect the information. In addition, it will defeat an argument that some information lost its trade secret status as a result of being shared with the third party. Oftentimes, employers may want to share sensitive information as part of the hiring process. An employer may want to use an NDA with potential employees to create a legally enforceable mechanism to keep that information from being shared with others.

The example of Sage and Dana is certainly a case where a confidentiality agreement would have been useful. Indeed, employees are not likely to take or disclose something if they know that an employer considers the information confidential, and even more so in the case where they have made a promise to keep it secret. A legally enforceable contract provides an avenue for recovery in the case of disclosure. Although an employer always has the ability to pursue a claim for the theft of its information, it is a far easier proposition when it can show an acknowledgment that the information is protectable and a promise to safeguard it.

Confidentiality agreements are the type of agreement that employers may want to use for all of their workers who could potentially come into contact with sensitive information that the employer would want to protect. Employers may find that there are few, if any, employees who would not meet this requirement. Even the most junior entry-level employee likely has access to something that could endanger a business if it fell into the wrong hands.

What can be difficult, however, is determining that information has been taken in the first place. In the example of Sage and Dana, Sage had a clear trail of Dana's activity, but that is not always the case. The employee may take information in much more surreptitious ways, such that even if an electronic trail is left, it may be difficult to discover or what is even lost when temporary log files are discarded from the computer system.

Even if an employer is sure that an employee has taken some of its confidential information, a lack of a clear trail may be all that is necessary to defeat the employer's claim. We expect people to be honest and own up to what they have done, but experience shows that honesty is more of an aspiration than a reality. Employees may lie about what they have done or take steps to cover their tracks and delete the evidence, making proving claims difficult and expensive. Agreements are a useful tool for employers, but on their own they are seldom enough and should be paired with systems to control and monitor access to sensitive information.

## Non-Competes

There may be times when the breadth of what the business would like to protect is so great or so resistant to specific definitions or categorization that the business may want to use a non-compete agreement to protect it. These agreements limit a former employee's ability to engage in activities that are in competition with their former employer for some period after the employment relationship ends. An employee subject to such an agreement will not be able to take what they know about the employer's customers and use that knowledge to siphon off work or make sales. A former employee will not be able to utilize his training in the specialized sphere in which the business operates to build the success of its competitors.

Since non-competes are so useful, it is no wonder that employers like them. It is also not surprising that they have been used in ways that go beyond the employer's interests in protecting its information and business and have, instead, been used as a way to keep employees from leaving their current jobs and improving and developing their careers. Therefore, policymakers and courts are suspicious of and have imposed restrictions on their use to ensure that they are not abused. Indeed, these suspicions have led to efforts at the federal level to ban non-compete agreements in their entirety. In fact, in 2024, the Federal Trade Commission (FTC) put forth a rule that declared most non-competes to be unenforceable. However, a federal court in Texas struck down this rule shortly before it was scheduled to go into effect on the basis that the FTC had exceeded its authority. Time will tell whether that decision will hold or be overturned. Either way, this is an ongoing issue that employers should continue to pay attention to. It is expected that attempts to rein in non-competes will continue and that they will continue to face significant opposition.

For now, at least, non-competes are allowed in most states, although several states have banned them entirely. Within most of the United States, either by statute or by court action, steps have been taken to ensure that non-competes are not abused. All states require that non-competes be "reasonable." Reasonable non-competes are those that are appropriately limited in scope, duration, and geography and that are designed to be no greater than is necessary to protect the legitimate business interests of employers.

For a non-compete agreement to be sufficiently limited in scope, it must not restrict the employee from doing work that he was not doing for the employer. So, an employer that sold only lumber could not restrict an employee from working to sell other building materials. After all, an employer does not have any interest in stopping a former employee from doing things that could not possibly have any effect on the employer's business.

Despite some surges in the use of non-competes in recent years, where they have been used for positions ranging from CEO to sandwich-maker, their use should really be restricted to those employees that constitute high-level competitive threats to the business. Indeed, recent attempts, including those by the Federal Trade Commission, to limit the use of non-competes or to prohibit them entirely are borne out of the observation that, rather than being used for those high-level people, they are pervasive throughout some industries without regard to whether the employee poses a competitive threat. What is important to remember is that non-competes must be designed to protect those legitimate business interests that employees could affect rather than as leverage to effectively keep employees trapped in their positions because they will be unable to accept work elsewhere. If someone breaches a non-compete, the employer may find that achieving a remedy is difficult. When you have put an agreement in place to protect your business, and someone fails to live up to what they have promised to do, in order to recover, you will need to show that your business was actually harmed. Unfortunately, when that harm involves the loss of customer accounts, some passage of time is necessary to establish that harm occurred. Indeed, unless someone tells you about a former employee's activities, you may not even know that the agreement has been breached until long into the future when the finances of the business are ultimately impacted.

The upshot for leaders is that non-competes can be a useful tool (where allowed) but must be reasonable. Non-competes can be difficult to enforce, practically speaking, but a reasonable restriction will fare much better.

## Non-Solicitation Agreements

In cases where what an employer seeks to protect consists of information about its customers or employees, it may want to consider a non-solicitation agreement. If written properly, these agreements are not necessarily subject to the same restrictions as non-competes but can be a valuable way to safeguard relationships. An employer can require that, for a reasonable period of time after leaving employment, a former employee be prohibited from soliciting, for business or employment, those customers or employees that the former employee has a personal relationship with by virtue of their previous employment. These agreements keep employees from using the goodwill that they developed for the purpose of benefiting their employer for their own purposes and for the purposes of other employers. Where these agreements are limited to those people with whom the former employee has personally interacted, courts are less likely to question their use and more likely to conclude that the interests protected by them are within what the employer is legally entitled to protect. One difficulty of drafting this type of agreement is that, often, a former employee may not even be aware of what customers he or she worked with. Therefore, employers wishing to use non-solicitation agreements should provide a way to discover information about who they are prohibiting the former employee from soliciting.

In contrast to the skepticism that courts express regarding non-competes, properly written non-solicitation agreements are generally allowed. Businesses may want to use these agreements for those customer-facing employees, such as salespeople, who, although not high-level employees, nevertheless, could use personal relationships developed on the employer's behalf to siphon away business.

Going back to the example of Sage and Dana, if Dana had been subject to a non-solicitation agreement, Sage would have been in a much better position to respond when Dana began soliciting Sage's customers. Just knowing that doing so would breach her agreement with Sage may have been enough to keep Dana from reaching out to these people. And, if Dana chose to breach the agreement, Sage would have a much better chance of stopping the behavior by informing Dana's new employer of the existence of the agreement and, if necessary, suing Dana for damages caused by the loss of the business of those customers improperly solicited.

## Takeaways Regarding the Protection of Business Information

Employers have a wide range of tools available to them to protect secrets associated with their businesses. But, in order for them to be effective, businesses need to first be clear about what they are protecting and why and then use tools available to them to do just that. The time to worry about your confidential information is before the opportunities for disclosure occur, not after they have already passed. If you have employees that, because of their positions or their access to your secret information, have the potential to harm your business if things go awry, you need to plan for the worst and protect your own information and information that has been entrusted to you. Here are a few ideas on how to do so:

- Update policies to ensure employees know what documentation is deemed confidential, proprietary, and/or trade secret information.

- Consider having employees sign confidentiality agreements.

- Consider non-solicitation agreements in order to safeguard clients and to prevent employees from leaving and taking clients with them.

- Consider non-compete agreements (if allowed where your business operates) and whether high-level executives should be asked at the time they are hired to enter into one.

- Take reasonable measures to safeguard confidential information, pay special attention to personal cell phone usage, remote workers, and information that can be copied from computer systems.

# Conclusion

There you have it—a number of key concepts that just might keep you out of court! Whether you read this entire book from front to back or simply cherry-picked a handful of problematic areas, you are to be congratulated for increasing your knowledge of key areas that keep employment lawyers like us busy.

Remember, this book tracks federal law, and state law may impose additional requirements. That makes it extra important for you to develop some local resources, whether that's a local law firm or local human resource consultant, to keep you up to date if you have questions or to go to if a problem arises.

Also, know that the law is constantly changing and evolving. Although we have tried to focus on significant concepts that have been around for a long time (in some cases, decades), it is important that you monitor changes in the law that could impact your business. As we have seen this year, new rules and legal guidance for employers have been rolled out at an unprecedented rate, so be on the lookout for more changes. There are many easy resources to use to make sure you are kept up to date. Many law firms (including ours) maintain blogs/email updates, so if a change occurs, you will be notified. It is easy to subscribe to our blog (or others), so that is one way to stay on top of it. Another great resource to monitor is the EEOC. They have emails they send out with significant announcements, ones that tell you what type of cases they are pursuing, and ones that highlight what type of guidance they are issuing. Go to EEOC.gov to find out more about email updates you can receive.

As we have discussed, though, it is not enough for one individual in an organization to stay up to date. Instead, all leaders and supervisors need some level of training to stay out of court. We are striving to provide resources on that front at lawforleaders.com. There are certainly other resources, too. Your local law firm may have some, and your local human rights commission or agency may provide some options, too.

At any rate, we hope to never see you in court and wish you and your business much success!

# About the Authors

## Pam Howland

Pam Howland has been practicing law in Boise, Idaho, for twenty-four years. After graduating from Gonzaga University School of Law in 2000, Pam moved to Boise, Idaho, where she clerked for the Idaho Supreme Court and then spent sixteen years working in litigation and employment law for a large regional firm.

In 2016, Pam saw a need in the market—employers needed affordable and competent legal counsel who could assist them with employment counseling issues, compliance questions, and defense strategies against claims and lawsuits. Pam started Idaho Employment Lawyers to fill that gap.

As the years went by, Pam noticed several patterns emerging. First, Pam witnessed firsthand how miserable it was for employers to get hauled into court. Between the cost, the uncertainty, and the stress, it became clear that if there was any way to avoid the judicial system altogether, every effort should be made to achieve that goal.

Second, Pam noticed that nearly every claim and lawsuit could have been avoided if supervisors and other leaders would have devoted some time and energy into learning key compliance concepts. Pam started Law for Leaders in 2023 to provide a resource for employers to accomplish this goal. Pam wrote this book as part of her continuing mission to help employers stay out of trouble, to become better leaders, and to learn basic compliance concepts that every leader must know to supervise people and to effectively run a business.

## Doug Plass

Doug Plass holds a Juris Doctorate, magna cum laude, from the University of Idaho College of Law and a Master of Science from the University of California at Davis. While in law school, Doug got a taste of employment law during an internship with Idaho Employment Lawyers and has not looked back.

Prior to working in the legal profession, Doug spent more than two decades working in the hospitality industry as a chef, a caterer, and eventually as a restaurant owner. Doug has a wealth of experience working firsthand through issues many employers face by building his businesses from the ground up and doing all the things small business owners find themselves doing, from marketing to cleaning floors.

In Doug's legal career, he has focused on assisting clients in navigating employment law challenges, including discrimination complaints, whistleblower actions, and working through employment agreements and policies. Doug uses his extensive experience as an entrepreneur to understand the challenges facing employers of all sizes and to help them respond with solutions that fit their unique circumstances. Doug currently lives in Idaho with his family and a couple of cattle dogs.

## Benjamin T. Cramer

Benjamin T. Cramer joined Idaho Employment Lawyers, PLLC in 2020 after a fifteen-year career in higher education, including seven years working in legal education. Ben's career and educational journey has included stops in Salem, OR, Philadelphia, PA, Spokane, WA, Athens, GA, and Boise, ID – which has helped him gain an appreciation for both the diversity and shared experiences within workplaces and communities throughout the U.S. Over the course of his career, Ben has adjudicated numerous matters through a variety of administrative processes, drafted various policies and procedures, and counseled and advised individuals and groups through challenging conflicts. Ben's practical experience complying with and implementing Title IX, Title VI, the ADA, and internal policies, provides him with a unique understanding and perspective to the issues facing employers.

Ben's practice focuses on helping employers navigate the inherent challenges of an expanding and changing workforce, primarily in relation to the Idaho Human Rights Act, Title VII, the ADA, Fair Labor Standards Act, and performance management.

Ben obtained his Juris Doctor, cum laude, from the University of Georgia School of Law and possesses a Master of Arts degree in Organizational Leadership from Gonzaga University. Ben grew up in rural eastern Oregon (Burns) and received his B.A. from Willamette University in Salem, OR. He is licensed to practice law in Idaho and Oregon. Ben's previous legal experience includes work for a now-retired general practitioner based in eastern Oregon and internships with the Ada County Prosecuting Attorney's Office and the Oregon Court of Appeals. Ben currently resides in Meridian, Idaho with his wonderful wife, daughters, and extended family.

## Jennifer M. Walrath

Jennifer Walrath has a Juris Doctorate, cum laude, from the Georgetown University Law Center. While in law school, her writing and analytical abilities earned her a seat on the Georgetown Journal of Law and Public Policy, where she was an editor and published an article. While in law school, Jennifer also participated in the school's Federal Legislation Clinic and had the great opportunity to work on proposed legislation that ultimately was enacted as the Americans with Disabilities Act Amendments of 2008. As it turns out, that was Jennifer's first taste of employment law, and now, years later, she is an employment lawyer!

In the early years of her career, Jennifer worked for national and global law firms in Washington, D.C., gaining valuable experience in complex litigation and government investigations. She has seen firsthand the costs and stresses of protracted litigation, as well as the costs of failures in compliance. After relocating to Idaho, Jennifer focused her practice on employment defense.

In her work with Idaho Employment Lawyers, Jennifer works directly with employers, getting to know their business and people, and crafting policies, procedures, and best practices to fit operational and compliance needs. Jennifer also provides counseling on terminations, discipline, and other employment decisions, all with the goal of helping employers identify and resolve issues early. Jennifer currently lives in Idaho, and spends as much time as she can with her family and enjoying the great outdoors.

www.ingramcontent.com/pod-product-compliance
Lightning Source LLC
Chambersburg PA
CBHW062035200326
41519CB00017B/5039